ExcelTips

Excel 2010 Conditional Formatting

Compiled from the pages of ExcelTips, *your free weekly productivity newsletter*

Excel 2010 Conditional Formatting

Published by:

Sharon Parq Associates, Inc.
PO Box 794
Orem, UT 84059

Produced and published in the United States of America

Revision history:

1 Apr 2011: First published

Table of Contents

Introduction

Virtually everyone knows that you can use Excel to store and calculate values. Just about as many people also know that you can format the information stored in a worksheet. You can control all sorts of ways that the information in a cell (or range of cells) is displayed—change the font size, the weight of the font, the color used, how many decimal places it uses, its alignment in the cell, and on and on.

What if you wanted the way that a cell appears to be based on some condition, however? For instance, you might want the text in a cell to be bold if the value is above some threshold or you might want the typeface to be red if the value is negative. This is where conditional formatting comes into play—the application of formats based upon criteria that you specify.

The conditional formatting capabilities of Excel are impressive and can be very powerful. All you need to do is picture how you want your data to appear, and then figure out the criteria that should be met in order for the formatting to be applied. Whenever the values change on which your conditional formatting is based, Excel changes the formatting to reflect those changed values.

To make conditional formatting even more powerful, Excel allows you to define multiple criteria to be applied to a cell or range of cells. Each criterion can have different formatting characteristics associated with that criterion. Thus, you could have one criterion that applies if a value is under a lower threshold, one that applies if the value is between the lower threshold and an upper threshold, and a third that applies if the value is over the upper threshold.

The way in which you can use conditional formatting is limited only by your imagination. Excel allows most of its formatting power to be applied based on the criteria that you dream up. In ***Excel 2010 Conditional Formatting*** you'll find plenty of information about conditional formatting, but it is not the dry, lifeless information you'll often find in computer books.

Brought to you by the publisher of ***ExcelTips,*** your free weekly productivity newsletter, ***Excel 2010 Conditional Formatting*** zeroes in on what you need to know to understand and put conditional formatting to work right away. You'll also find ideas on how to make conditional formatting fit your needs. You'll discover ways to stretch your knowledge and enhance how you can present the data in your worksheets.

The information presented in ***Excel 2010 Conditional Formatting*** is organized into a collection of bite-sized "tips" that have appeared in various issues of ***ExcelTips.*** But there is more, because some of the information contained here has never appeared in any issue of ***ExcelTips.*** All in all you'll find the most up-to-date and complete information available anywhere relative to conditional formatting.

A Word about Versions

As the title of this e-book implies, ***Excel 2010 Conditional Formatting*** is designed to work with Excel 2010. The reason is simple: The latest release of Microsoft's spreadsheet program has operational differences—some subtle and some major—from earlier versions of Excel. These differences can affect the way that conditional formatting is handled.

The instructions and screen shots used in this e-book were all created using a Windows 7 system with Excel 2010 installed. As you compare what is on your screen with what you see in this e-book, don't be surprised if there are small, cosmetic differences. If you run across discrepancies of a more serious nature (I don't think you will), I'd love you to e-mail me with the details. Send your message to allen@sharonparq.com.

If you are using an earlier version of Excel and you want to discover how to better use conditional formatting, check the Tips.Net store and you can find a version of this e-book designed specifically for you.

Need More Tips?

If you want to stay in top Excel form, consider subscribing to ***ExcelTips.*** Your subscription is free; all you need is an e-mail account and you can receive a weekly dose of tips related to Excel. To subscribe, just visit the ***ExcelTips*** Web site:

http://excelribbon.tips.net

ExcelTips is part of the Tips.Net network, a collection of websites designed to bring you helpful tips, tricks, and ideas that can save you time, effort, and money. You can see the full breadth of the Tips.Net network by visiting our website:

http://www.tips.net

Sharing this E-Book

There was a lot of work that went into putting this e-book together. That means that this information has value, and your friends, neighbors, and co-workers may want to share it.

The information in this e-book is copyrighted. Please do not share this information with others—you purchased ***Excel 2010 Conditional Formatting*** and you have a right to use it on your system. Another person who has not purchased this e-book does not have that right. It is the sales of this valuable information that makes the continued publishing of ***ExcelTips*** possible. If enough people disregard that simple economic fact, the newsletter will no longer be viable or available.

If you work for a company and your company purchased this e-book, remember that they purchased it for you. Just because a company purchases an e-book does not give the company the right to share that e-book with all their employees. (Think about it—does purchasing a book at the bookstore give the company the right to photocopy it for each of their employees? No, it does not.)

If your friends and coworkers think this information is valuable enough to ask you for it, they should think it is valuable enough to purchase on their own. After all, the price is low enough that just about anyone should be able to afford a copy.

It should go without saying that you cannot post this e-book or the information it contains on any electronic bulletin board, Web site, FTP site, newsgroup, or … well, you get the idea. The only place from which this e-book should be available is the ***ExcelTips*** Web site. If you want an original copy, visit the Tips. Net store at the following address:

http://store.tips.net/

1

Conditional Formatting Basics

Defining a Single Condition

Excel includes a powerful feature that allows you to format the contents of a cell based on a set of conditions that you specify. This is known as ***conditional formatting.*** How you define conditional formats depends on whether you want to define a single formatting condition or multiple conditions. Even if you decide you want to define multiple conditions, however, it is beneficial to understand how single conditions are defined.

The first step in using conditional formatting, of course, is to select the cell whose formatting should be conditional. Then, with the Home tab of the ribbon displayed, click Conditional Formatting in the Styles group. Excel displays a list of various conditions you can define:

- **Highlight Cells Rules.** These rules are designed to allow you to indicate how a specific cell should be highlighted, based on the condition you specify.
- **Top/Bottom Rules.** These rules are used to format cells based on whether they are in the upper or lower portion of a range of values.
- **Data Bars.** These rules allow you to specify a graphic bar that appears based on the value in a cell. (Similar to a histogram, where longer bars denote larger values and shorter bars are used for lesser values.)
- **Color Scales.** These rules are used to indicate a range of colors that should apply to a cell, based on the value in that cell.

- **Icon Sets.** These rules allow you to apply various graphic icons based on the condition you specify.

In reality, each "condition" selected from these options is nothing but a shortcut to filling in the settings of the New Formatting Rule dialog box. You may have noticed that each of the above choices leads to a series of specific conditions (just hover the mouse pointer over the choice to see the conditions) and that the last condition, in all cases, is "More Rules." If you select this option, if you select one of the defined conditions, or if you select New Rule (available when you first click Conditional Formatting) you will typically see the New Formatting Rule dialog box.

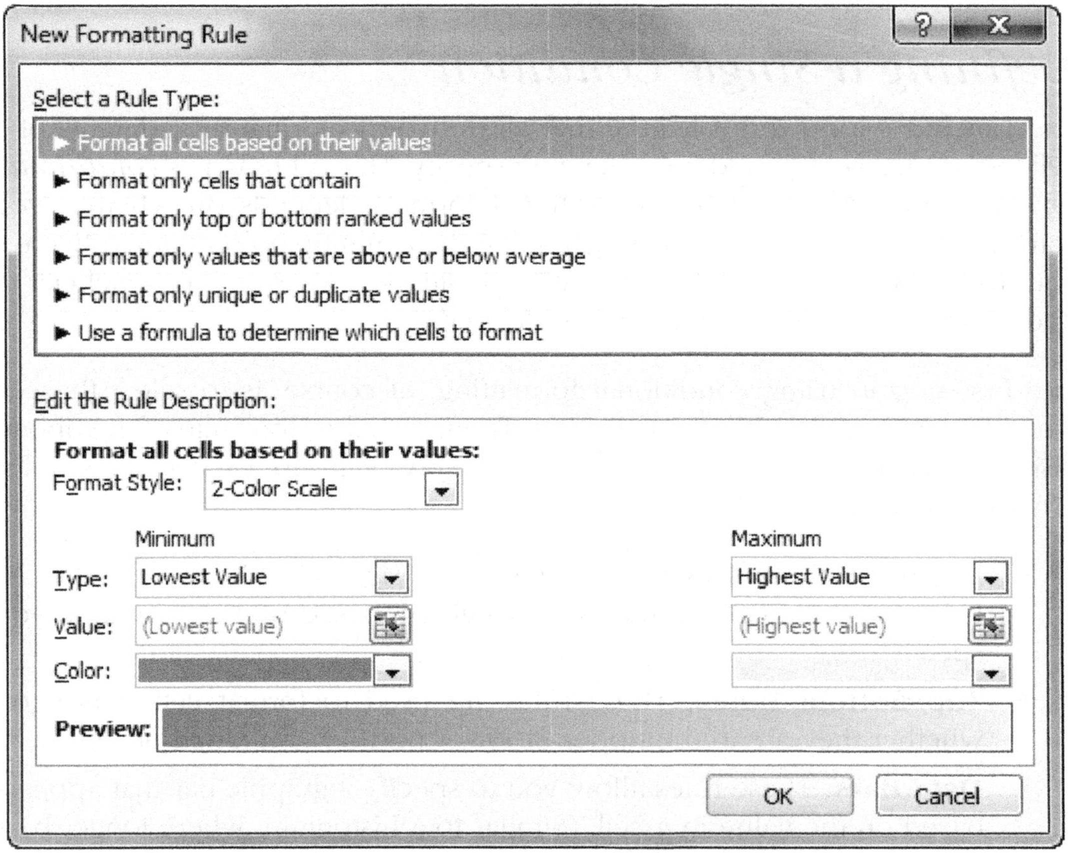

The New Formatting Rule dialog box.

In the top of the dialog box you select a type of rule you want applied to the selected cells. There are six rule types:

- Format All Cells Based On Their Values
- Format Only Cells that Contain
- Format Only Top or Bottom Ranked Values
- Format Only Values that are Above or Below Average
- Format Only Unique or Duplicate Values
- Use a Formula to Determine which Cells to Format

These six rule types may look somewhat familiar; they are the basis for the pre-defined rules discussed earlier in this tip. When you select a rule type, Excel changes the settings you can make in the bottom of the dialog box. Each rule type has value, but you will find, over time, that the last rule type (where you use a formula to define formatting) is the most powerful.

When you select a rule type and then adjust the settings in the bottom of the dialog box, you can (depending on the rule type) click the Format button to specify the formatting Excel should apply if the conditions detailed in the rule are satisfied. How you set up rules and apply formatting is the basis for all the information in the rest of this e-book.

When you are satisfied with your rule settings and formatting options, you can click OK to dismiss the New Formatting Rule dialog box. The format is applied and you can continue working in your worksheet.

Working with Multiple Conditions

When working with conditional formats, you'll often discover times when you need to apply multiple conditions to a single cell. The previous tip discussed how to define a single condition to apply to a cell, but Excel allows you to define many conditions that can all apply to the same cell or range of cells.

Begin by selecting the cells for which you want to define conditional formatting rules. Then, with the Home tab of the ribbon displayed, click Conditional

Formatting in the Styles group. From the resulting list of options, select Manage Rules. Excel displays the Conditional Formatting Rules Manager.

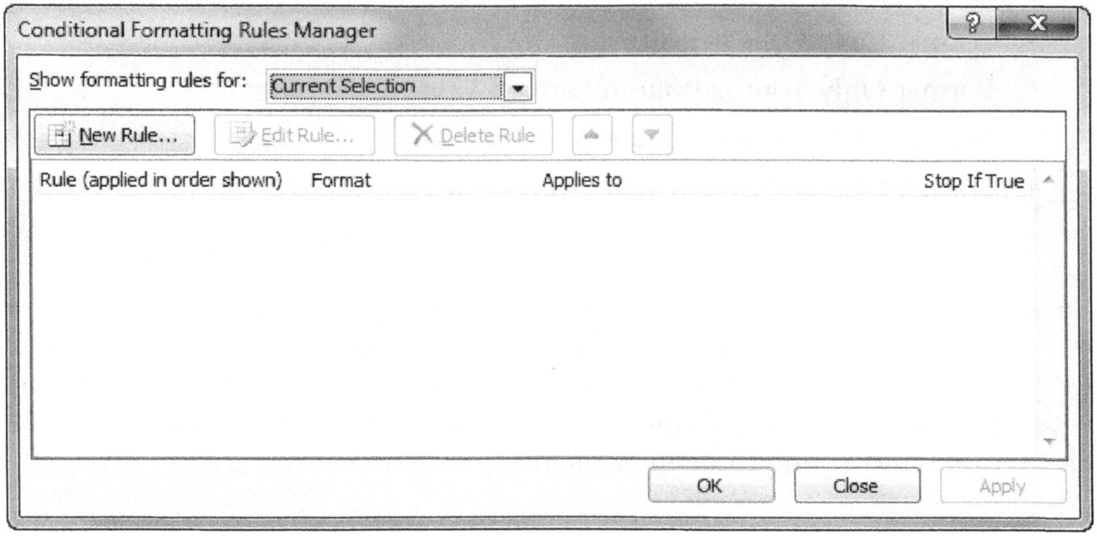

The Conditional Formatting Rules Manager

The Conditional Formatting Rules Manager is nothing but a list of the rules which have been defined for the selected cells. Each rule is shown on a separate line, and you can work with the rules by clicking one of the available buttons:

- **New Rule.** Allows you to define a new rule, which is added to the end of the rules list. Defining a new rule uses the same procedures described in the previous tip.
- **Edit Rule.** Make changes to the selected rule.
- **Delete Rule.** Remove the selected rule so it no longer applies to the selected cells.
- **Up Arrow.** Move the selected rule up in the list of rules.
- **Down Arrow.** Move the selected rule down in the list of rules.

Rules are always evaluated in the order in which they appear in the Conditional Formatting Rules Manager. You can modify the evaluation order by using the up and down arrow tools.

More than Three Conditional Formats

Long-time users of Excel understand that, historically, you were limited to only three conditions when setting up conditional formatting. This limitation was removed in Excel 2007 and you can now set up many more than three. You can use the Conditional Formatting Rules Manager to define as many conditional formats as you need. Just follow these general steps:

1. Select the cell or cells to which you want the conditional formats applied.
2. Make sure the Home tab of the ribbon is displayed.
3. Click the Conditional Formatting tool in the Styles group. Excel displays a drop-down list of options.
4. Click the Manage Rules option. Excel displays the Conditional Formatting Rules Manager dialog box.

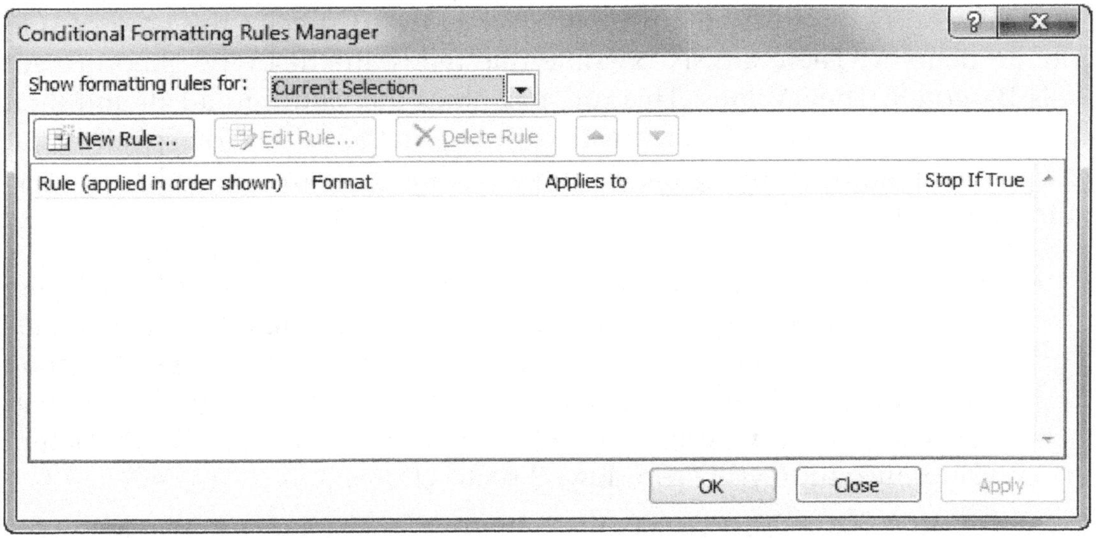

The Conditional Formatting Rules Manager dialog box.

5. Click the New Rule option. Excel displays the New Formatting Rule dialog box, which you can use to define rules as you desire.
6. At the top of the dialog box, specify the type of rule you are defining.

7. If appropriate for the type of rule you are creating, click the Format button. Excel displays the Format Cells dialog box, which you can use to specify the formatting associated with the conditional format.
8. Click OK to dismiss the Format Cells dialog box.
9. Click OK to dismiss the New Formatting Rule dialog box.
10. Repeat steps 5 through 9 to define as many rules as necessary.
11. Click the up and down arrows to move the rules you created to the order in which they should be evaluated.
12. Click OK to dismiss the Conditional Formatting Rules Manager dialog box.

Defining a Rule Based on Cell Values

When you display the New Formatting Rule dialog box (see earlier tips for information on how to do this), Excel allows you to specify the type of rule you are defining. There are six possible rule types; the first type is Format All Cells Based On Their Values. This rule examines the values in a cell and then applies color, a data bar, or an icon set based upon the value. You specify what Excel should apply by using the Format Style drop-down list, which consists of these options:

- **2-Color Scale.** You specify the minimum and maximum for the scale, along with the color for the minimum and maximum. Excel then applies a gradation between those two colors depending on where the value falls in the scale between minimum and maximum. Excel also allows you to specify different ways of determining the minimum and maximum values; use the Type drop-down lists to choose.
- **3-Color Scale.** You specify the minimum, midpoint, and maximum for the scale, along with the colors to be used for all three. Excel then applies a gradation from one color to the next, depending on where the value in the cell falls on the scale. Excel also allows you to specify different ways of determining the minimum, midpoint, and maximum values; use the Type drop-down lists to choose.

- **Data Bar.** Excel creates a "bar" that represents where the cell value occurs on a scale from lowest to highest. Excel provides different ways to specify the value for the shortest and longest bars; just use the Type drop-down lists to choose.
- **Icon Sets.** Using the Icon Style drop-down list, you specify which type of icon set you want used to represent the values in the cells. Each set consists of 3, 4, or 5 icons, and you specify the thresholds Excel should use in determining which of the icons to display.

Defining a Rule Based on Cell Contents

When you display the New Formatting Rule dialog box (see earlier tips for information on how to do this), Excel allows you to specify the type of rule you are defining. There are six possible rule types; the second type is Format Only Cells That Contain. This type of rule is designed to format a cell based upon the attributes of the contents of the cell.

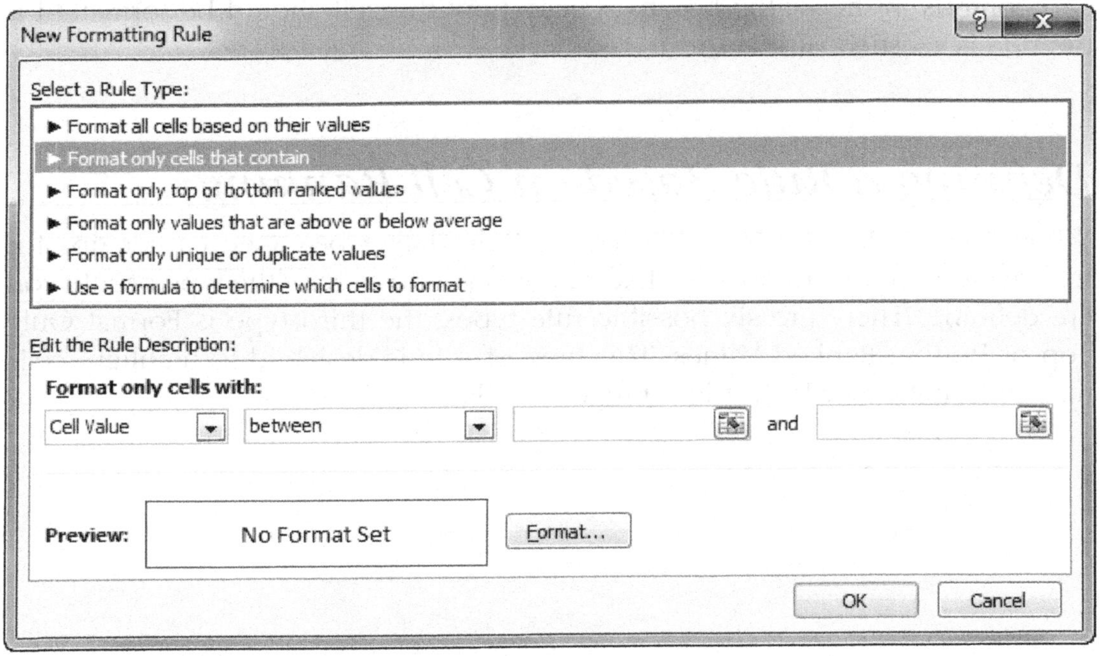

The New Formatting Rule dialog box.

Use the first drop-down list, at the left of the dialog box, to specify one of the following options:

- **Cell Value.** Allows you to indicate the relationship of the cell to specific thresholds.
- **Specific Text.** Allows you to indicate text that the cell must contain, must not contain, begins with, or ends with.
- **Dates Occurring.** Allows you to indicate various date ranges (yesterday, last week, last month, etc.) to which the cell value can be compared.
- **Blanks.** The cell contains no values, formulas, or errors.
- **No Blanks.** The cell is not empty.
- **Errors.** The cell contains an error value.
- **No Errors.** The cell does not contain an error value.

The idea is to pick a rule option that allows Excel to analyze the data in each cell that you are formatting. Regardless of the option you select, you can click the Format button to display the Format Cells dialog box. You can use the tabs and controls in the dialog box to specify how the cell should be formatted if the rule is satisfied (if it is true).

Defining a Rule Based on Cell Ranking

When you display the New Formatting Rule dialog box (see earlier tips for information on how to do this), Excel allows you to specify the type of rule you are defining. There are six possible rule types; the third type is Format Only Top or Bottom Ranked Values. This type of rule is designed to highlight cells that rank highest or lowest in a range of cells.

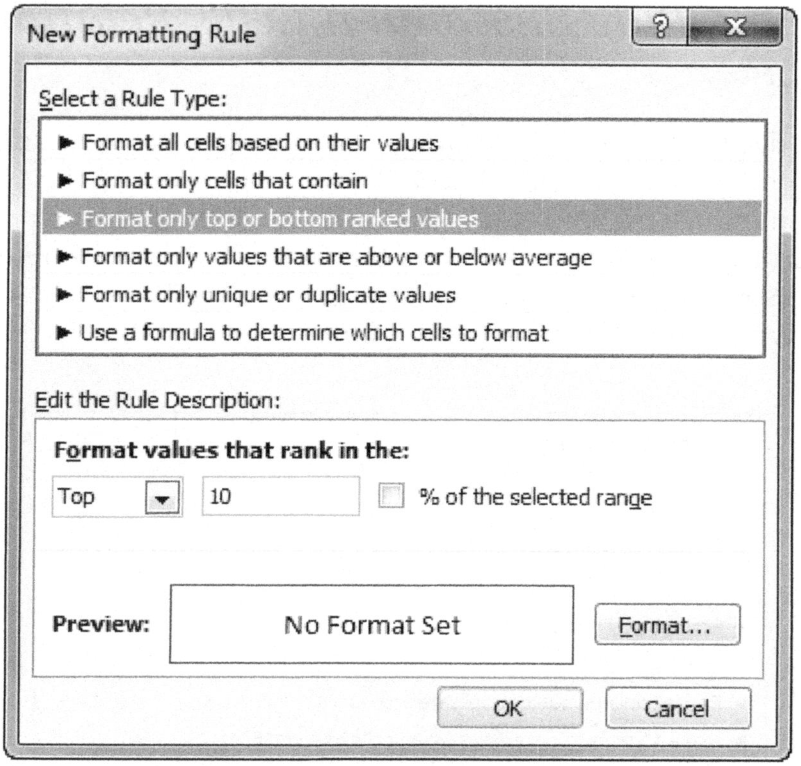

The New Formatting Rule dialog box.

You should make sure that you have more than a single cell selected when you define this type of rule. It is these cells that make up the data set from which ranking is determined. Using the left-most drop-down list you can select Top or Bottom, and then use the next box to indicate what number or percentage you want to qualify as satisfying the rule. (Clicking the % check box indicates whether the value you enter is a percentage. If not checked, then the value is interpreted as a regular number.)

With your rule criteria set, you can click the Format button to display the Format Cells dialog box. You use the tabs and controls in the dialog box to indicate how the cell should be formatted if the rule is satisfied.

Defining a Rule Based on a Cell's Relation to Average

When you display the New Formatting Rule dialog box (see earlier tips for information on how to do this), Excel allows you to specify the type of rule you are defining. There are six possible rule types; the fourth type is Format Only Values That Are Above or Below Average. This type of rule evaluates a cell relative some statistics derived from a group of cells, so you should only set up this type of rule if you first start with a range of cells selected.

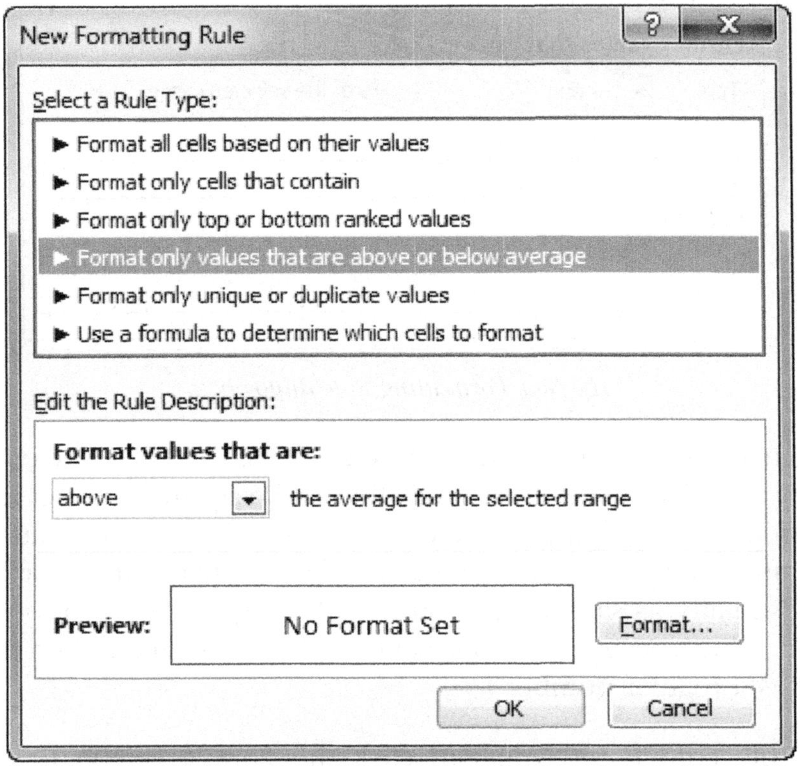

The New Formatting Rule dialog box.

Using the left-most drop-down list, choose Above, Below, or some other statistical determination relative to the average of the selected cells. (You can select, for instance, 2 standard deviations above or below the average.) You can then click the Format button to display the Format Cells dialog box where you indicate how the cell should be formatted if the cell fits the criteria you specified.

Defining a Rule Based on Duplicate Status

When you display the New Formatting Rule dialog box (see earlier tips for information on how to do this), Excel allows you to specify the type of rule you are defining. There are six possible rule types; the fifth type is Format Only Unique or Duplicate Values. This rule type is designed to be used on a range of cells; make sure you select the range before defining the rule.

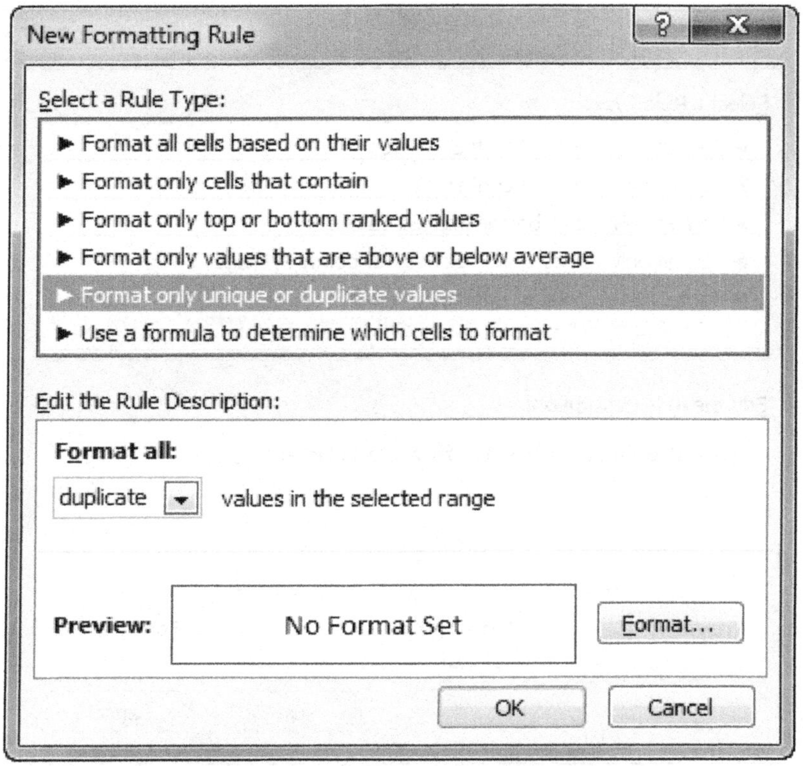

The New Formatting Rule dialog box.

There are only two options available in the left-most drop-down list: Duplicate and Unique. Each of the values in the selected range is compared to the others, and depending on whether the value duplicates others (if you choose

Duplicate) or is unique (if you choose Unique) the specified formatting (click the Format button) is applied to the cell.

Defining a Rule Based on a Formula

When you display the New Formatting Rule dialog box (see earlier tips for information on how to do this), Excel allows you to specify the type of rule you are defining. There are six possible rule types; the sixth type is Use a Formula to Determine which Cells to Format. If this type of rule is specified, then there is only a single box in the rule criteria.

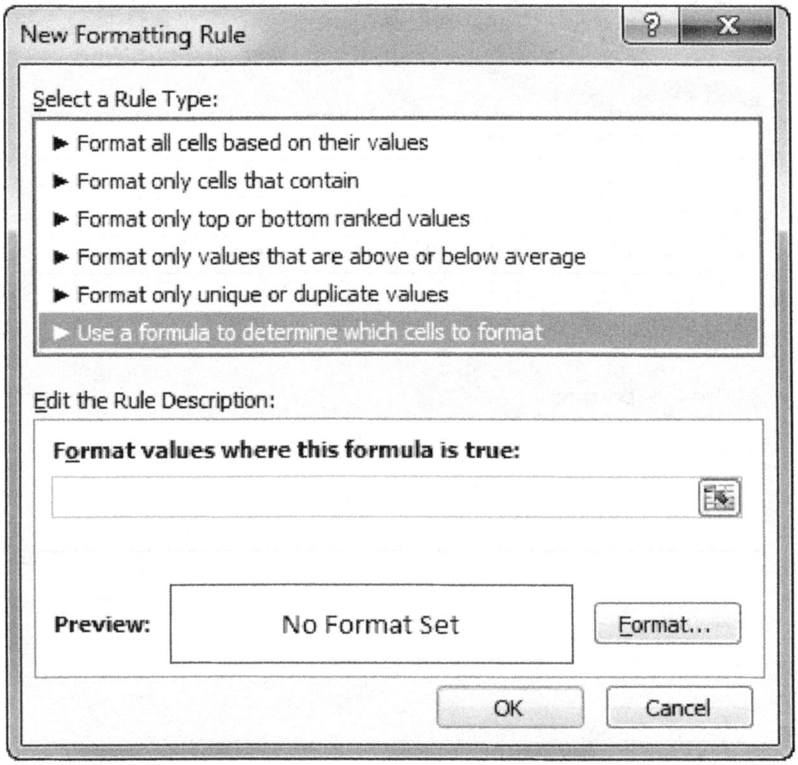

The New Formatting Rule dialog box.

In the box you can specify a particular formula for determining if special formatting should be applied to the cell. This is most useful if the formatting is based on a value in a cell different from the one to which you are applying the formatting.

For instance, let's say that column A has a list of company names and column N has a total of all the purchases made by that company during the year. You may want the company name to appear in bold, red type if their sales exceeded a certain amount. This type of scenario is perfect for using a formula for your conditional test. The reason is because the formatting in column A will be based not on column A, but on a value in column N.

Formulas must evaluate to either a true or false condition, not to some other value. For instance, you could use the formula **=N4>500** if you wanted cell A4 to be conditionally formatted if cell N4 exceeds a value of 500.

Copying Conditional Formatting

In Excel, conditional formatting is considered part of the regular formatting of a cell. If you want to copy conditional formatting from one cell to another, you can do so by simply copying the cell and pasting it (or its format) to another cell. If you want to copy a conditional format to a range of cells (and only the conditional format), the easiest way to do so is by following these general steps:

1. Select the cell that contains the conditional format you want copied.
2. Display the Home tab of the ribbon.
3. In the Styles section, click Conditional Formatting. Excel displays various options related to conditional formatting.
4. Click Manage Rules. Excel displays the Conditional Formatting Rules Manager. The format you want copied should already be filled in.

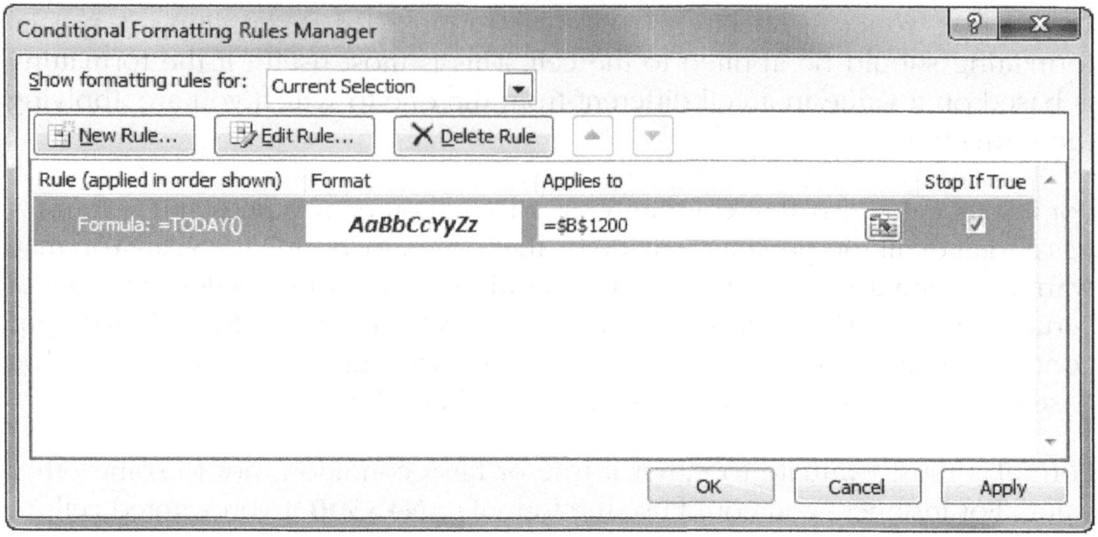

The Conditional Formatting Rules Manger.

5. Select whatever appears in the Applies To box.
6. Using the mouse, click and drag to select the range of cells to which the conditional format should be applied.

That's it. Excel does the rest and copies the conditional formatting, as you desired.

Deleting Conditional Formats

After you've applied a conditional format to a cell, you may have a need to later delete that format so that the cell is treated (and formatted) normally by Excel. Unfortunately, how you delete conditional formats may not be immediately obvious to you.

Conditional formats, to Excel, are just like any other format. That means that you can delete them by simply deleting all the formatting in a cell. Follow these steps:

1. Select the cell or cells whose formatting you want to delete.
2. Display the Home tab of the ribbon.
3. In the Editing group, click Clear | Clear Formats.

That's it. All the formatting is removed from the cells, including any conditional formatting. If you don't want to delete any explicit formatting in the cell, but instead want to delete just the conditional formats, follow these steps:

1. Select the cells from which you want to delete the conditional formatting.
2. Display the Home tab of the ribbon.
3. In the Styles section, click Conditional Formatting. Excel displays various options related to conditional formatting.
4. Choose Clear Rules | Clear Rules from Selected Cells.

If you don't want to delete all the conditional formatting rules, then you need to follow these steps, instead:

1. Select the cells from which you want to delete the conditional formatting.
2. Display the Home tab of the ribbon.
3. In the Styles section, click Conditional Formatting. Excel displays various options related to conditional formatting.
4. Click Manage Rules. Excel displays the Conditional Formatting Rules Manager.

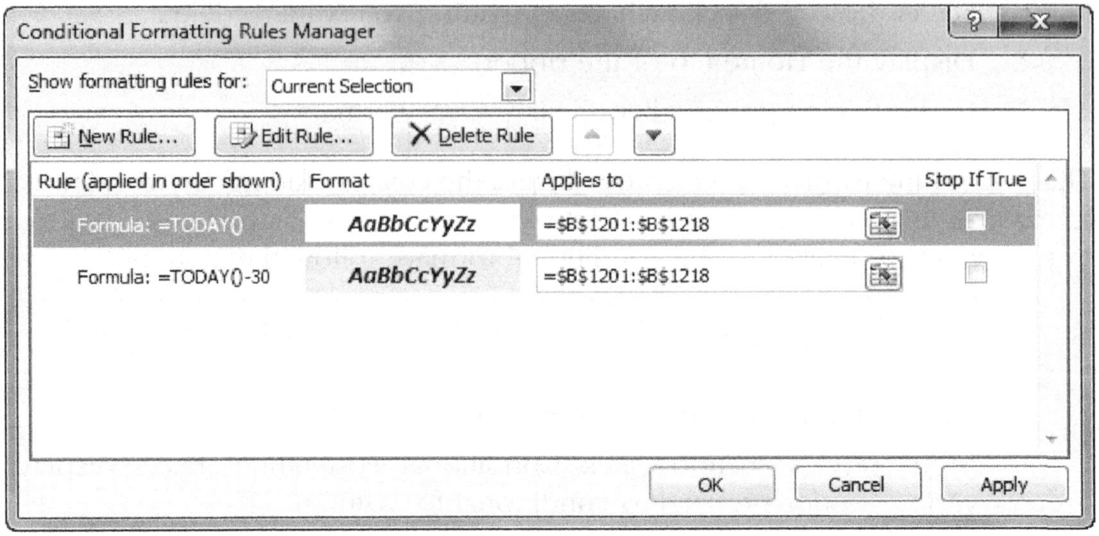

The Conditional Formatting Rules Manger.

5. From the list of available rules, select the one you want to delete.
6. Click Delete Rule.
7. Repeat steps 5 and 6 for any other rules you want to delete from the selected cells.
8. Click OK to close the Conditional Formatting Rules Manager dialog box.

Finding Cells Containing Conditional Formats

When you inherit a worksheet from someone, you may want to discover which cells have conditional formatting applied to them. This is rather easy to do using the Go To feature of Excel. Follow these steps:

1. Press **F5**. Excel displays the Go To dialog box.
2. Click Special. Excel displays the Go To Special dialog box.

The Go To Special dialog box.

3. Select the Conditional Formats radio button.
4. Make sure the All radio button is selected. (The radio button becomes accessible when you select the Conditional Formats radio button.)
5. Click OK.

That's it. Excel selects all the cells in the current worksheet that have conditional formatting applied to them.

Losing Formatting

Jennifer is in an office with ten people, all using either Excel 2007 or Excel 2010. Several of them have intermittent problems with losing formatting. The formatting includes fonts, colors, shading, borders, number formats, and so on.

They save and close the workbook; the next time they open it, the formatting is gone. They can't find a pattern, and were wondering if this is a known problem.

There is no acknowledgement from Microsoft that it is a known problem (at least, as far as we can find), but it apparently is a problem shared by many people. As far as we can tell, the problem could be due to two different potential causes.

First, you should make sure that your workbook is being saved in native Excel 2007/2010 format. If you are saving it in the older Excel 97-2003 format, then it is possible that the losses you are seeing are due to the formatting not being supported in the older format. This is particularly true with colors and conditional formatting.

The other possible cause is that the workbook file is corrupted in some manner. The solution is to transfer your data from the current workbook to a new workbook and then see if the problem occurs in the new one.

Protecting Conditional Formatting

Larry wrote about a problem he was encountering with protecting a worksheet he developed. He has cells that contain both formulas and conditional formatting. He can protect both of them in a worksheet, but if someone selects a cell and copies it to another worksheet, the conditional formatting is visible.

When you copy a protected cell from one sheet to another, if the formulas in the source cell were hidden in the protection process, then the results of the formulas are pasted, unprotected, into the target cells. This is probably no big deal, as you wanted the formulas—not the results—protected.

Excel is not as protective about conditional formats, however. The conditional formats of the cells that you paste, since they are in an unprotected worksheet, can be viewed and modified, as desired. This can be a problem if the conditional formats contain formulas that you want to also keep private.

The only way around this problem is to disable the ability to copy anything from your protected worksheet. You do this through the use of a macro, added to the worksheet object, that would disable copying.

```
Private Sub Worksheet_Deactivate()
    Application.CutCopyMode = False
End Sub
```

This macro works because anytime the worksheet is deactivated (meaning, the target worksheet is selected), then CutCopyMode is set to False. This results in the "marching ants" that appeared around the source cells when the user pressed **Ctrl+C** being removed, and pasting is therefore no longer possible. Copying and pasting on the same worksheet is still fine, just not to a different (unprotected) worksheet.

Detecting Errors in Conditional Formatting Formulas

Allan uses a lot of conditional formatting, nearly always using formulas to specify the conditions for the formatting. Recently he discovered, by chance, that he had a #REF! error in one of his conditional format formulas. As far as Allan could figure, this was the result of deleting the row of a cell referred to in the formula. The impact is that the conditional formatting won't work for that condition. This has made Allan concerned that there are other instances of conditional formats that have become corrupted since originally being set up. He wonders if there is any simple way of checking all conditional formatting so that these errors can easily be found.

The best way is to use a macro to step through all the conditional formats defined for a worksheet. The following macro does just that, looking for any #REF! errors in the formulas.

```
Sub FindCorruptConditionalFormat()
    Selection.SpecialCells(xlCellTypeAllFormatConditions).Select
    For Each c In Selection.Cells
        For Each fc In c.FormatConditions
```

```
            If InStr(1, fc.Formula1, "#REF!", _
              vbBinaryCompare) > 0 Then
                MsgBox Prompt:=c.Address & ": " _
                  & fc.Formula1, Buttons:=vbOKOnly
            End If
        Next fc
    Next c
End Sub
```

If an error is found, then a message box displays both the address of the cell and the formula used in the conditional formatting rule.

2

Conditionally Formatting Cells

Coloring Cells with Formulas

Cells in a worksheet can contain values or they can contain formulas. At some time, you may wish to somehow highlight all the cells in your worksheet that contain formulas by coloring those cells. There are several ways you can approach and solve this problem. If you don't have a need to do the highlighting that often, a manual approach may be best. Follow these steps:

1. Press **F5**. Excel displays the Go To dialog box.
2. Click Special. Excel displays the Go To Special dialog box.

The Go To Special dialog box.

3. Select the Formulas radio button.
4. Click OK.

At this point, every cell in the worksheet that contains formulas is selected, and you can add color to those cells or format them as desired. This approach can be automated, if desired, by using a macro like the following:

```
Sub ColorFormulas()
    ActiveSheet.Cells.SpecialCells(xlCellTypeFormulas, 23).Select
    With Selection.Interior
        .ColorIndex = 6
        .Pattern = xlSolid
    End With
End Sub
```

You can run this macro as often as necessary in order to highlight the various cells that contain formulas. The only problem is that if a formula is deleted from a cell that was previously highlighted, the highlighting remains; it is not removed automatically. In this case, a different macro approach is mandated. This macro acts on a range of cells you select before running the macro.

```
Sub ColorFunction()
    For Each cell In Selection
        If cell.HasFormula Then
            With cell.Interior
                .ColorIndex = 6
                .Pattern = xlSolid
            End With
        Else
            cell.Interior.ColorIndex = xlNone
        End If
    Next cell
End Sub
```

The macro checks each cell in the range. If the cell contains a formula, then it is highlighted. If the cell does not contain a formula, then the highlight is turned off.

Another potential solution is to use a user-defined function along with the conditional formatting capabilities of Excel. Create the following function in the VBA Editor:

```
Function CellHasFormula(c As Range) As Boolean
    CellHasFormula = c.HasFormula
End Function
```

With this function in place, you can follow these steps:

1. Select the cells to which the conditional formatting should apply.
2. Display the Home tab of the ribbon.
3. Click the Conditional Formatting tool in the Styles group. Excel displays a list of conditional formatting options.
4. Choose New Rule. Excel displays the New Formatting Rule dialog box.
5. In the list of rule types, select Use a Formula to Determine which Cells to Format.

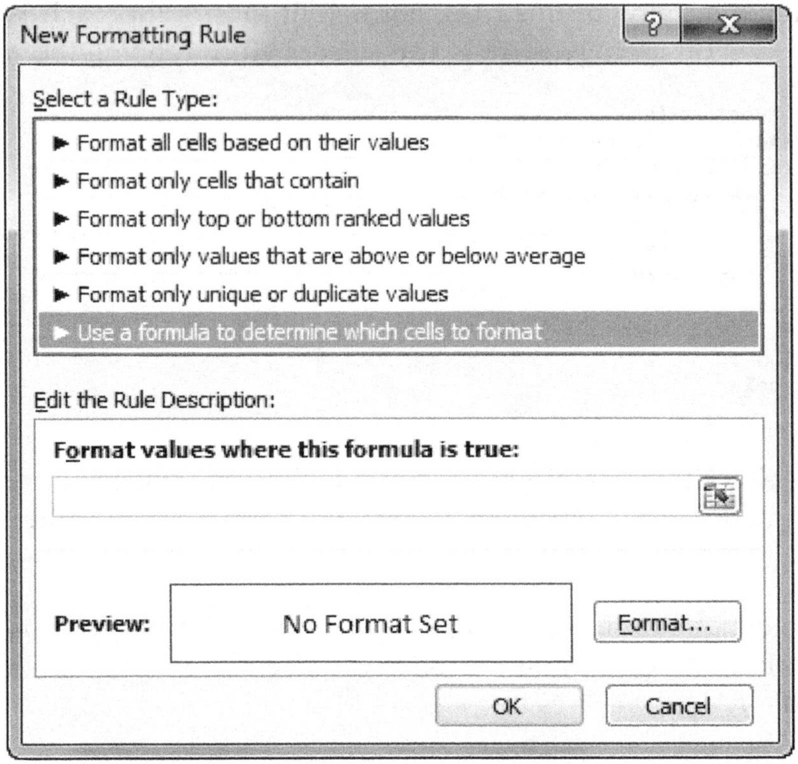

The New Formatting Rule dialog box.

6. In the box in the rule criteria area, enter the following formula:

```
=CellHasFormula(A1)
```

7. Click the Format button. Excel displays the Format Cells dialog box.

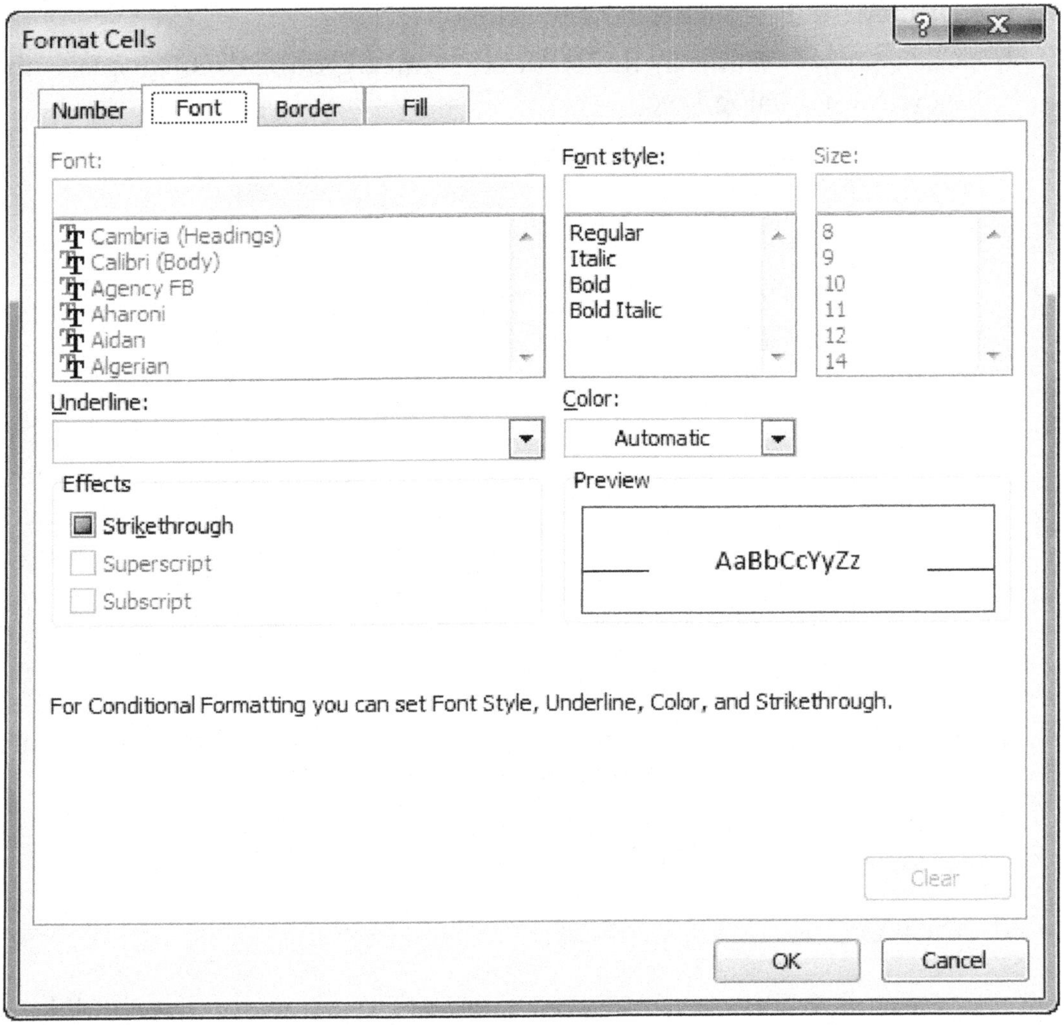

The Format Cells dialog box.

8. Change the formatting for the cells in any way desired.
9. Click OK to dismiss the Format Cells dialog box.
10. Click OK to dismiss the New Formatting Rule dialog box.

It is interesting to note that you don't have to create a VBA macro to use the conditional formatting route, if you don't want to. (Some people have a natural aversion to using macros.) Instead, you can follow these steps:

1. Display the Formulas tab of the ribbon.
2. Click Define Name in the Defined Names group. Excel displays the New Name dialog box.

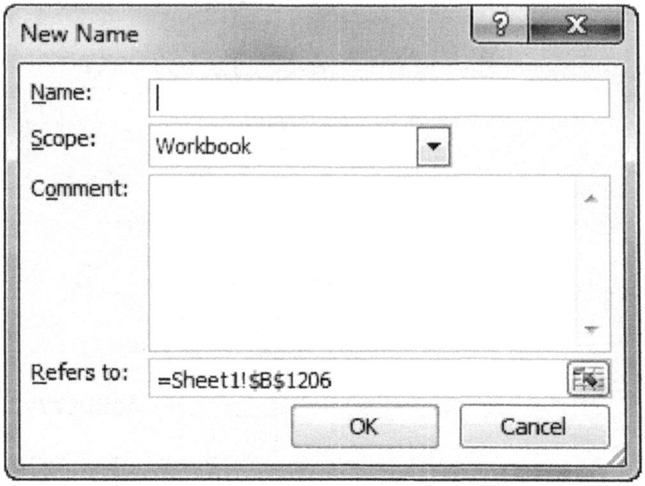

The New Name dialog box.

3. In the Name box, enter the name you want assigned to this formula. For this example, use **FormulaInCell**.
4. In the Refers To field enter the following:

```
=GET.CELL(48,INDIRECT("rc",FALSE))
```

5. Click OK.

Now, you can follow the steps previously outlined for setting up the conditional formatting. The only difference is in step 6, where you would enter the following formula:

```
=FormulaInCell
```

Shading a Cell until Something is Entered

When creating a worksheet in which information must be entered into specific cells, you may find it helpful to shade the cells if they are blank, but have the shading removed if something is entered into the cell. You can easily accomplish this task by using the conditional formatting feature in Excel. Follow these steps:

1. Select the cells to which the conditional formatting should apply.
2. Display the Home tab of the ribbon.
3. Click the Conditional Formatting tool in the Styles group. Excel displays a list of conditional formatting options.
4. Choose New Rule. Excel displays the New Formatting Rule dialog box.
5. In the list of rule types, select Format Only Cells that Contain.
6. Using the drop-down list at the left of the rule area, choose Blanks.

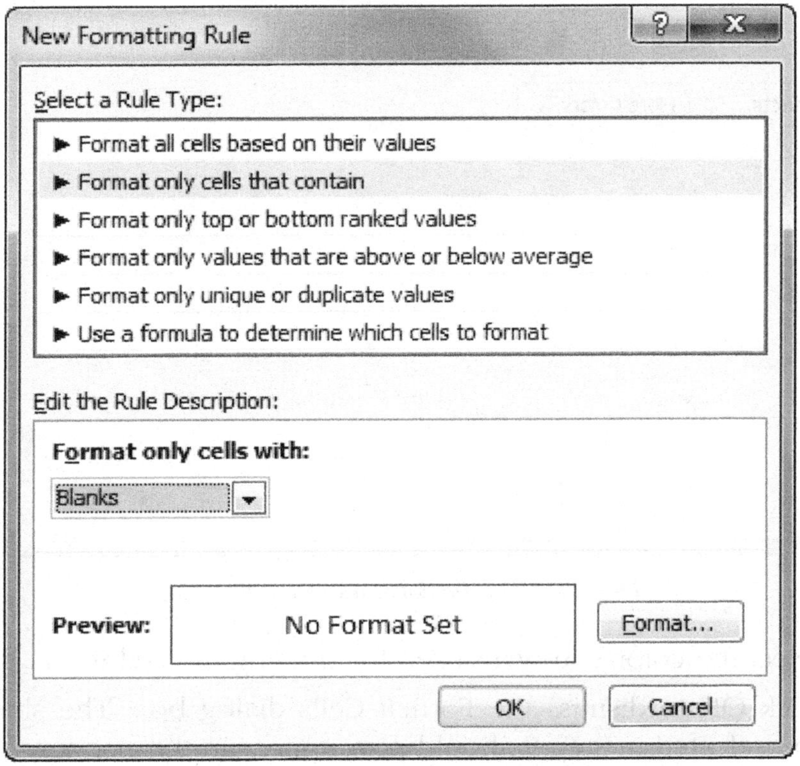

The New Formatting Rule dialog box.

7. Click Format to display the Format Cells dialog box.
8. Click the Fill tab.

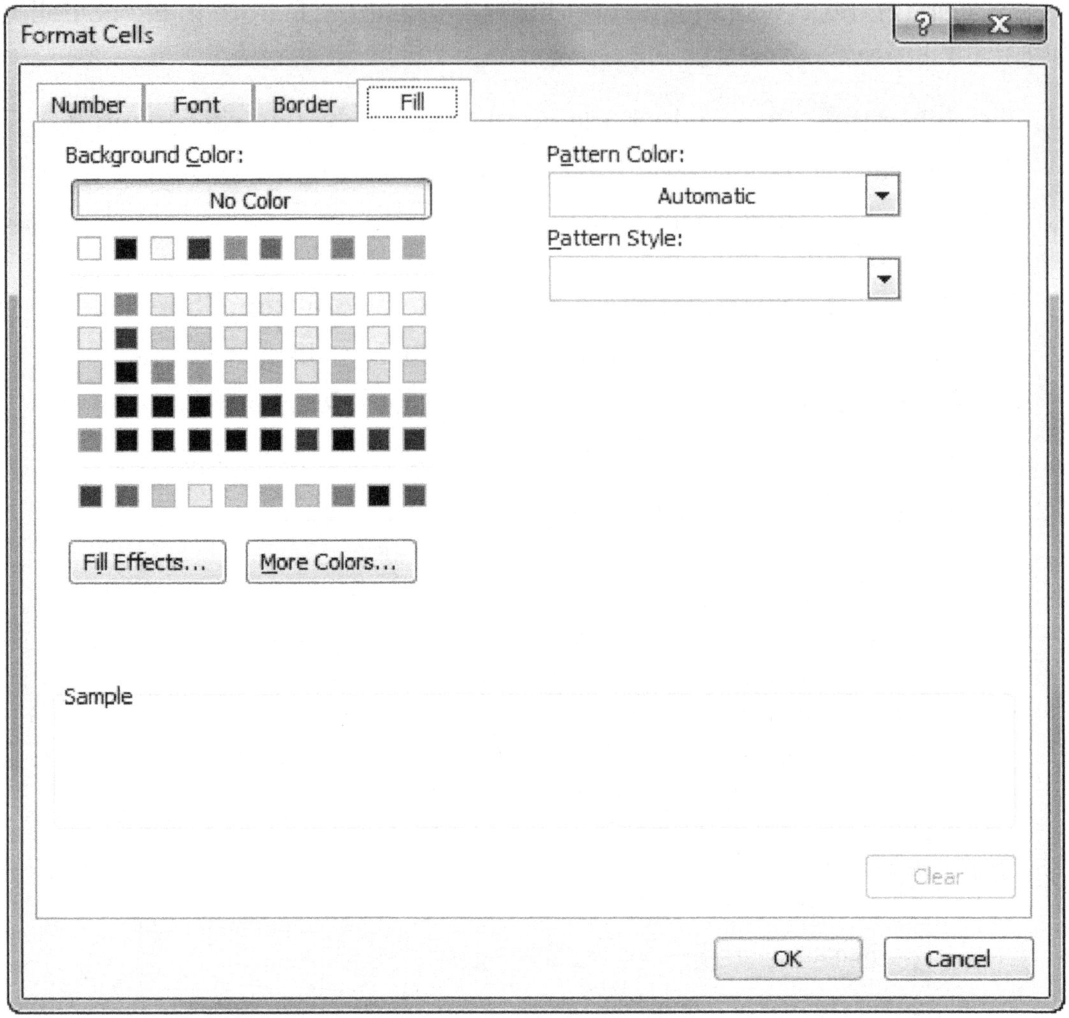

The Fill tab of the Format Cells dialog box.

9. Select the color you want used for shading the cell if it is blank.
10. Click OK to dismiss the Format Cells dialog box. The shading color you selected in step 9 should now appear in the preview area for the rule.
11. Click OK.

All the empty cells among those selected in step 1 should now appear shaded. When you enter something into one of the shaded cells, the shading should disappear.

Highlighting Values in a Cell

Trev has a table of sales forecasts by product that several users review and update. The forecasts are initially set with various formulas, but the users are allowed to override the formulas by entering a value into any cell that contains one of the formulas. If a user does this, it would be helpful for Trev to have Excel somehow highlight that cell.

There are a couple of approaches you can take. First, you could use conditional formatting to do the highlighting. Set the conditional formatting rule type to Format Only Cells that Contain, "Cell Value" "Not Equal To," and then enter the formula as the comparison. This will tell you when the value in the cell does not equal whatever the formula is, but a potential "gottcha" is if the person overrides the formula with the result of that formula. For instance, if the formula would have produced a result of "27" and the user types "27" into the cell.

Another possibility is to define a formula in a named constant and then use that named constant in a conditional format. Follow these steps:

1. Display the Formulas tab of the ribbon.
2. Click Define name in the Defined Names group. Excel displays the New Name dialog box.

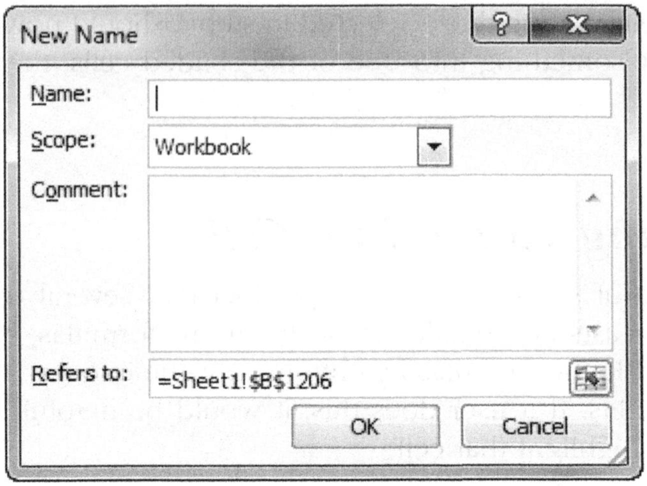

The New Name dialog box.

3. In the Name box, enter the name you want assigned to this formula. For this example, use **CellHasNoFormula**.
4. Select whatever is in the Refers To box, at the bottom of the dialog box, and press **DEL**. This gets rid of whatever Excel had there before.
5. Enter the following formula in the Refers To box:

```
=NOT(GET.CELL(48,INDIRECT("rc",FALSE)))
```

6. Click OK.

Now you can set up some conditional formats and use this named formula in the format. Simply set the conditional formatting rule type to Use a Formula to Determine which Cells to Format and enter the following formula in the condition:

```
=CellHasNoFormula
```

The formula returns True or False, depending on whether there is a formula in the cell or nor. If there is no formula, then True is returned and whatever format you specify is applied to the cell.

Another approach is to use a user-defined function to return True or False, and then set up the conditional format. You could use a very simple macro, such as the following:

```
Function IsFormula(Check_Cell As Range) As Boolean
    Application.Volatile
    IsFormula = Check_Cell.HasFormula
End Function
```

You can then specify the conditional formatting rule type as Use a Formula to Determine which Cells to Format and enter the following formula in the condition if, for instance, you are conditionally formatting cell C1:

```
=NOT(IsFormula(C1))
```

The formula returns True if there is no formula in the cell, so the conditional format is applied.

The only downside of using any of these formulas to determine if a formula is in the cell is that it cannot determine if the formula in the cell has been replaced with a different formula. This applies to both the macro approach and the defined formula approach.

A totally different approach is to rethink your worksheet a bit. You can separate cells for user input from those that use the formulas. The formula could use an IF function to see if the user entered something in the user input cell. If not, your formula would be used to determine a value; if so, then the user's input is used in preference to your formula. This approach allows you to keep the formulas you need, without them being overwritten by the user. This results in great integrity of the formulas and the worksheet results.

Highlighting Cells Containing Specific Text

You can use the conditional formatting feature in Excel to help draw attention to cells that contain specific text in which you are interested. For instance, if you have a range of cells and you want to know which ones contain the letters "shawn," then you can do the following:

1. Select the range of cells.
2. With the Home tab of the ribbon displayed, click the Conditional Formatting option in the Styles group. Excel displays a palette of options related to conditional formatting.

3. Choose New Rule. Excel displays the New Formatting Rule dialog box.
4. In the Select a Rule Type area at the top of the dialog box, choose Format Only Cells that Contain.
5. Using the left-most drop-down list in the criteria area, select Specific Text.

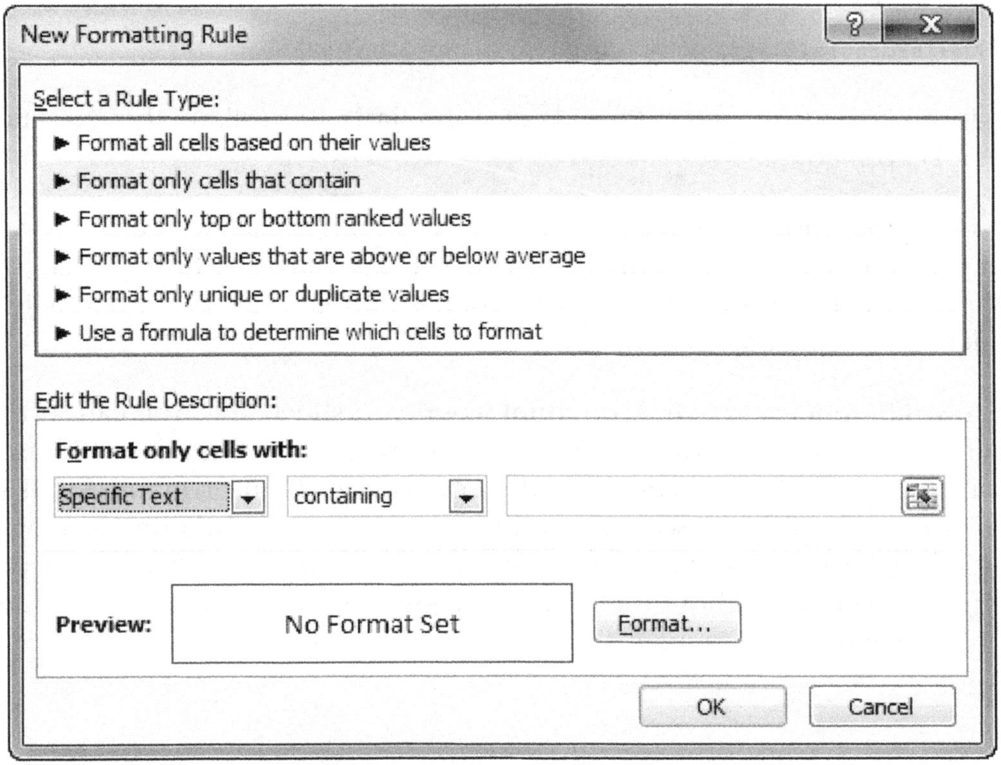

The New Formatting Rule dialog box.

6. Make sure the center drop-down list is Containing.
7. In the right-most box enter "shawn" (without the quote marks).
8. Click Format to display the Format Cells dialog box.
9. Using the controls in the dialog box, specify a format that you want used for those cells that contain the specified text. For instance, you may want bold text in a red typeface.

10. Click OK to dismiss the Format Cells dialog box. The formatting you specified in step 9 should now appear in the preview area for the rule.
11. Click OK.

Conditionally Highlighting Cells Containing Formulas

You probably already know that you can select all the cells containing formulas in a worksheet by pressing **F5** and choosing Special | Formulas. If you need to keep a constant eye on where formulas are located, then repeatedly doing the selecting can get tedious. A better solution is to use the conditional formatting capabilities of Excel to highlight cells with formulas.

Before you can use conditional formatting, however, you need to create a user-defined function that will return True or False, depending on whether there is a formula in a cell. The following macro will do the task very nicely:

```
Function HasFormula(rCell As Range) As Boolean
    Application.Volatile
    HasFormula = rCell.HasFormula
End Function
```

To use this with conditional formatting, select the cells you want checked, and then follow these steps:

1. With the Home tab of the ribbon displayed, click the Conditional Formatting option in the Styles group. Excel displays a palette of options related to conditional formatting.
2. Choose New Rule. Excel displays the New Formatting Rule dialog box.
3. In the Select a Rule Type area at the top of the dialog box, choose Use a Formula to Determine Which Cells to Format.

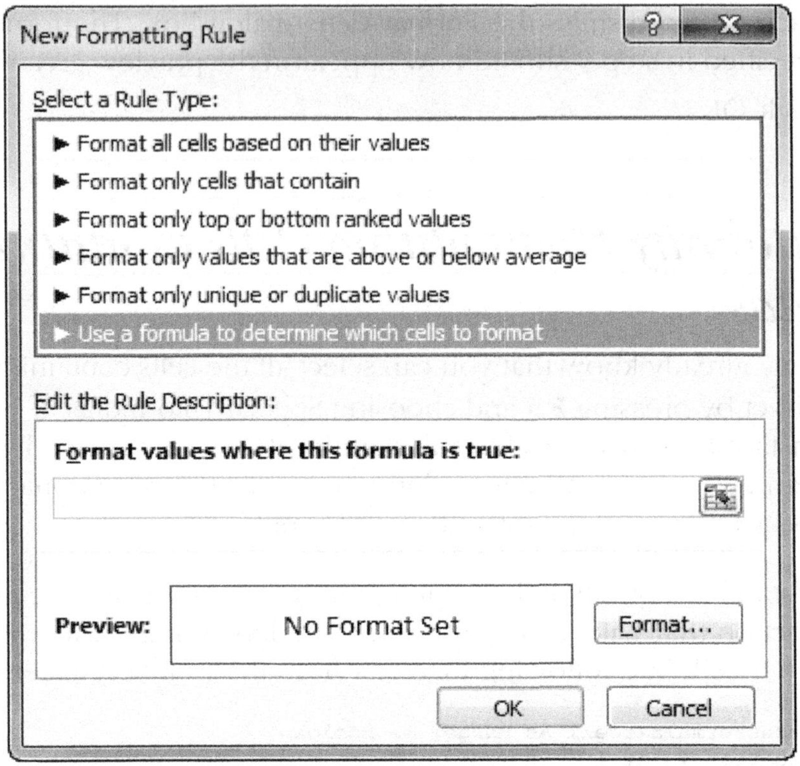

The New Formatting Rule dialog box.

4. In the Format Values Where This Formula Is True box, enter "=HasFormula(A1)" (without the quote marks). If the active cell in the range that you selected is not A1, you'll need to modify the formula slightly to reflect whatever cell is active.
5. Click Format to display the Format Cells dialog box.
6. Use the controls in the Format Cells dialog box to specify how you want the cells formatted.
7. Click OK to close the Format Cells dialog box.
8. Click OK.

Shading Based on Odds and Evens

If you have a series of values in a range of cells, you might want to use different formatting to differentiate the odd numbers from the even numbers. The way you do this is through the use of the Conditional Formatting feature in Excel. Follow these steps:

1. Select the cells that contain the odd and even values.
2. With the Home tab of the ribbon displayed, click the Conditional Formatting option in the Styles group. Excel displays a palette of options related to conditional formatting.
3. Click Manage Rules. Excel displays the Conditional Formatting Rules Manager dialog box.
4. Click New Rule. Excel displays the New Formatting Rule dialog box.
5. In the Select a Rule Type area at the top of the dialog box, choose Use a Formula to Determine Which Cells to Format.

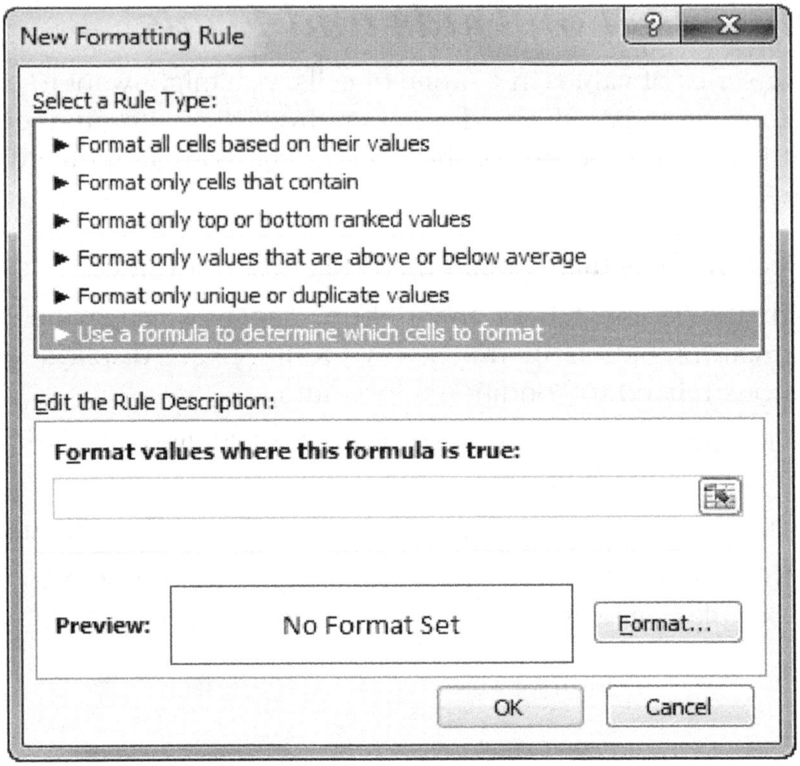

The New Formatting Rule dialog box.

6. In the Format Values Where This Formula Is True box, enter the following: =MOD(A1,2)-1. This formula will return True if the cell contains an odd value.
7. Click Format to display the Format Cells dialog box.
8. Using the controls in the dialog box, specify a format that you want used for those cells that contain an odd value.
9. Click OK to dismiss the Format Cells dialog box. The formatting you specified in step 7 should now appear in the preview area for the rule.
10. Click OK. The New Formatting Rule dialog box disappears and Excel again displays the Conditional Formatting Rules Manager dialog box. The rule you just defined is listed in the dialog box.
11. Repeat steps 4 through 10 for the second condition, but use the formula =MOD(A1,2)=0. This formula returns True if the cell contains an even value.

12. Click the up and down arrows to move the rules you created to the order in which they should be evaluated.
13. Click OK. Excel applies the conditional formatting to the cells you selected in step 1.

With this conditional formatting applied, if the cell is odd it will be one color and if even it will be another. If the cell contains text, the cell will be uncolored, meaning it will have the color of the cell before you added the conditional formatting. The conditional formatting overrides any formatting you put on the cell, so even if you try to change the cell color via the tools on the ribbons, the conditional formatting takes precedence.

The MOD function isn't the only thing you can use in your formula. If you want to determine whether the cell contains an odd value (step 6), you could use the following:

```
=ISODD(A1)
```

Similarly, if you want to determine if the cell contains an even value (step 11), you could use the following:

```
=ISEVEN(A1)
```

Displaying Negative Percentages in Red

It's easy using Excel's built-in number formats to display negative values in red. What isn't so obvious is how to display negative percentages in red. This is because Excel doesn't provide a built-in format that addresses this situation.

There are two distinct ways you can display negative percentages in red. One way is to use a custom number format. Precise details on how you put together custom formats has been covered in other issues of ***ExcelTips,*** so here is the quick way you can get the desired results:

1. Select the cell (or cells) that may contain negative percentages.
2. Display the Home tab of the ribbon.

3. Click the small icon at the lower-right corner of the Number group. Excel displays the Format Cells dialog box.
4. If the Number tab is not displayed, select it.
5. In the Category list, choose Custom. The dialog box changes so you can enter a custom format.

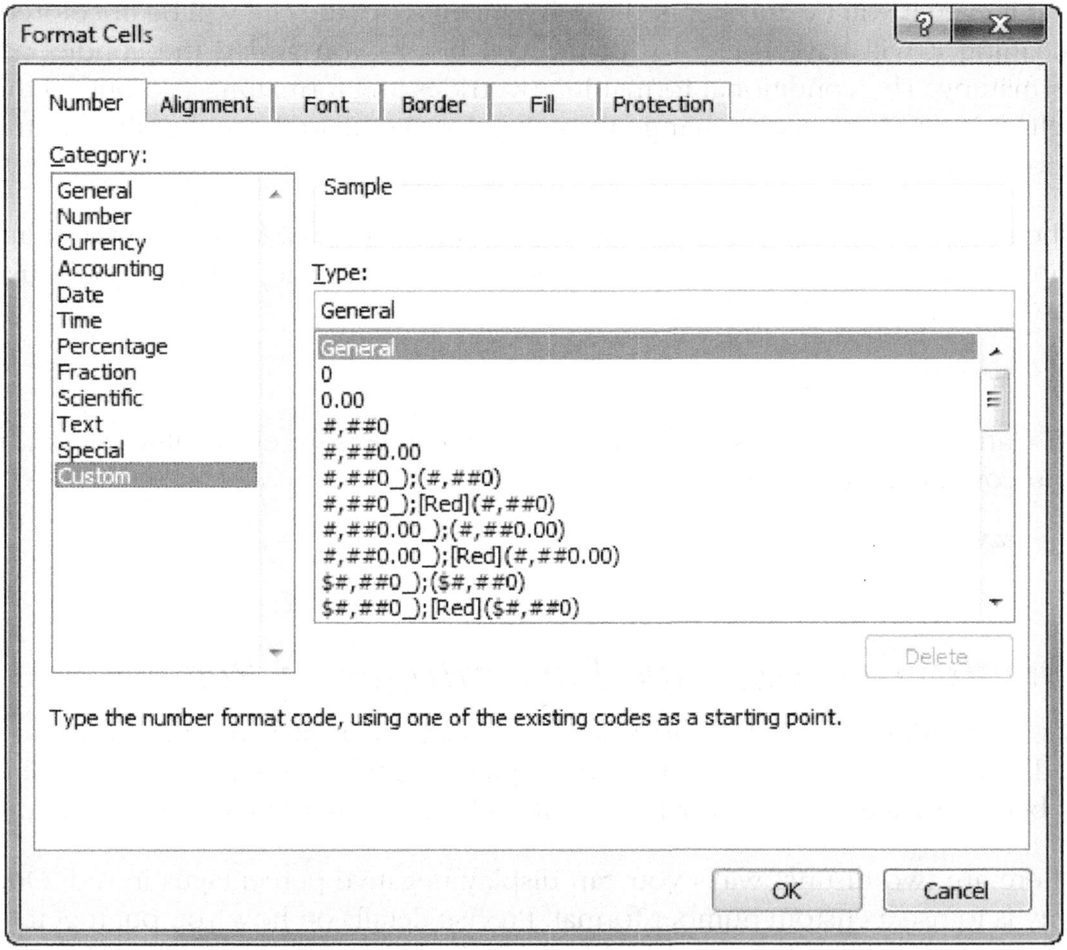

The Number tab of the Format Cells dialog box.

6. In the Type box, enter the following: 0.00%;[Red]-0.00%
7. Click OK.

The format you specify in step 6 displays positive percentages with two decimal places and displays negative percentages in red with two decimal places. (You can modify the number of decimal places in the format, if necessary.)

The other way that you can display negative percentages in red is to use conditional formatting by following these steps:

1. Select the cell (or cells) that may contain negative percentages.
2. With the Home tab of the ribbon displayed, click the Conditional Formatting option in the Styles group. Excel displays a palette of options related to conditional formatting.
3. Choose New Rule. Excel displays the New Formatting Rule dialog box.
4. In the Select a Rule Type area at the top of the dialog box, choose Format Only Cells that Contain.
5. Using the left-most drop-down list in the criteria area, select Cell Value. (This option may already be selected, by default.)
6. Make sure the center drop-down list is Less Than.

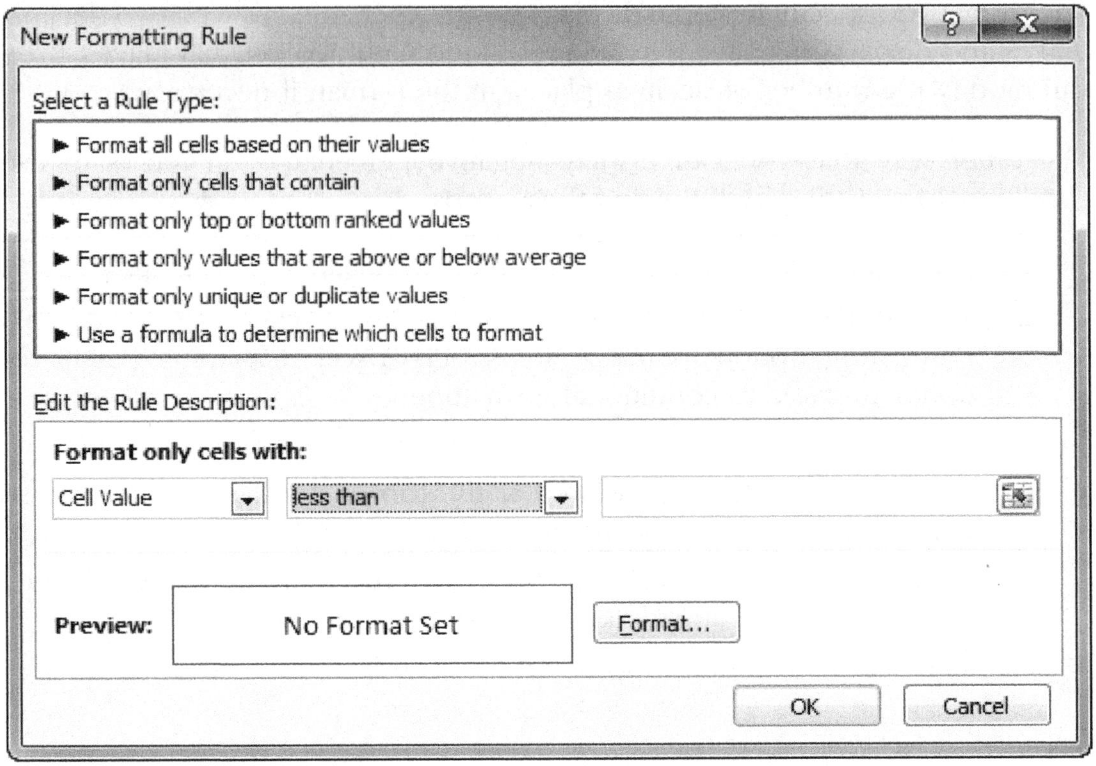

The New Formatting Rule dialog box.

7. In the box to the right of the second drop-down list, enter the numeral **0**.
8. Click Format. Excel displays the Format Cells dialog box with the Font tab selected.

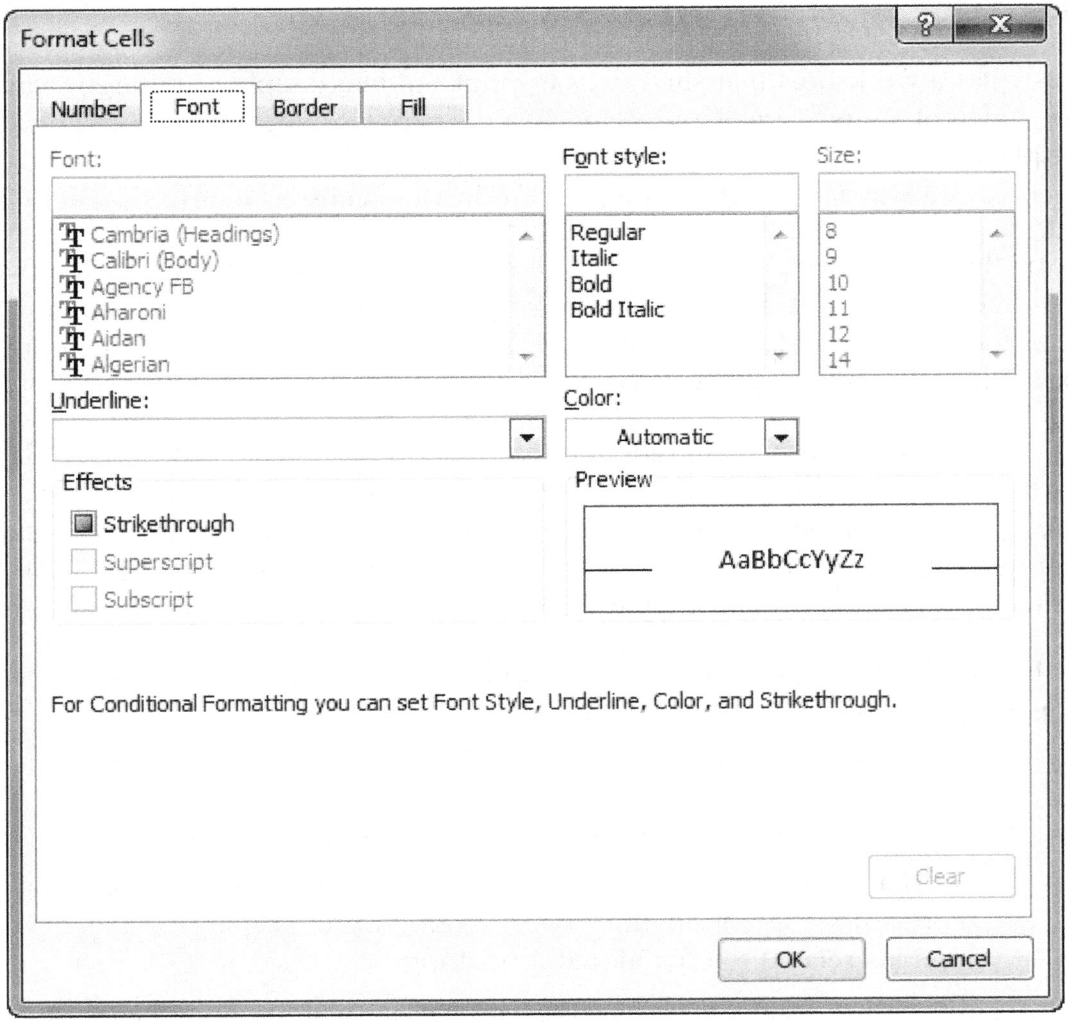

The Font tab of the Format Cells dialog box.

9. Use the Color drop-down list to choose the shade of red you want used for the negative percentages.
10. Click OK to close the Format Cells dialog.
11. Click OK to close the New Formatting Rule dialog.

Hiding Individual Cells

Ruby has a worksheet that she needs to print out in a couple of different ways for different users. Part of preparing her data for printing involves hiding or displaying some rows and some columns, as appropriate. Ruby wondered if there was a way to hide the contents of individual cells, as well.

If, by "hide," you want to have the cell disappear and information under it move up (like when you hide a row) or move left (like when you hide a column), then there is no way to do this in Excel. Actual hiding in this manner can only be done manually, on a row or column basis.

There are ways that you can hide the information in the cell, however, so that it doesn't show up on the printout. One easy way, for instance, is to format the cell so its contents are white. This means that, when you print, you'll end up with "white on white," which is invisible. Test this solution, though—some printers, depending on their capabilities, will still print the contents.

If this approach works for you, you could expand on it just a bit to make your data preparation tasks just a bit easier. Follow these general steps:

1. In an out-of-the-way cell (let's say it is cell J1) insert the letter "p."
2. Select the cell (or cells) you want to hide on the printout.
3. With the Home tab of the ribbon displayed, click the Conditional Formatting option in the Styles group. Excel displays a palette of options related to conditional formatting.
4. Click New Rule. Excel displays the New Formatting Rule dialog box.
5. In the Select a Rule Type area at the top of the dialog box, choose Use a Formula to Determine Which Cells to Format.

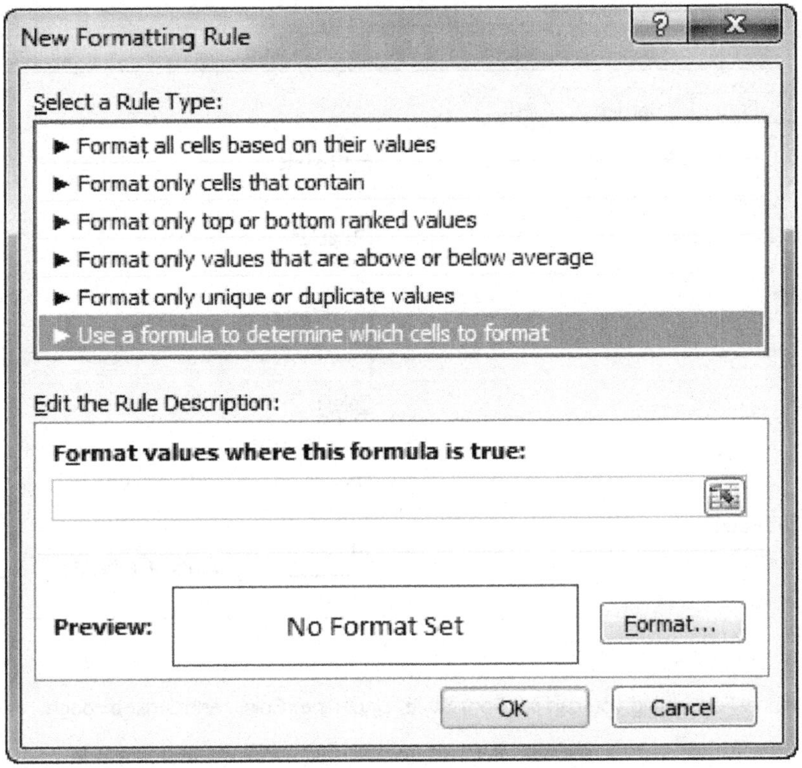

The New Formatting Rule dialog box.

6. In the criteria area for the rule enter the following: =J1="p". This formula will return True if the cell contains a lowercase letter "p."
7. Click the Format button. Excel displays the Format Cells dialog box.
8. Make sure the Font tab is displayed.

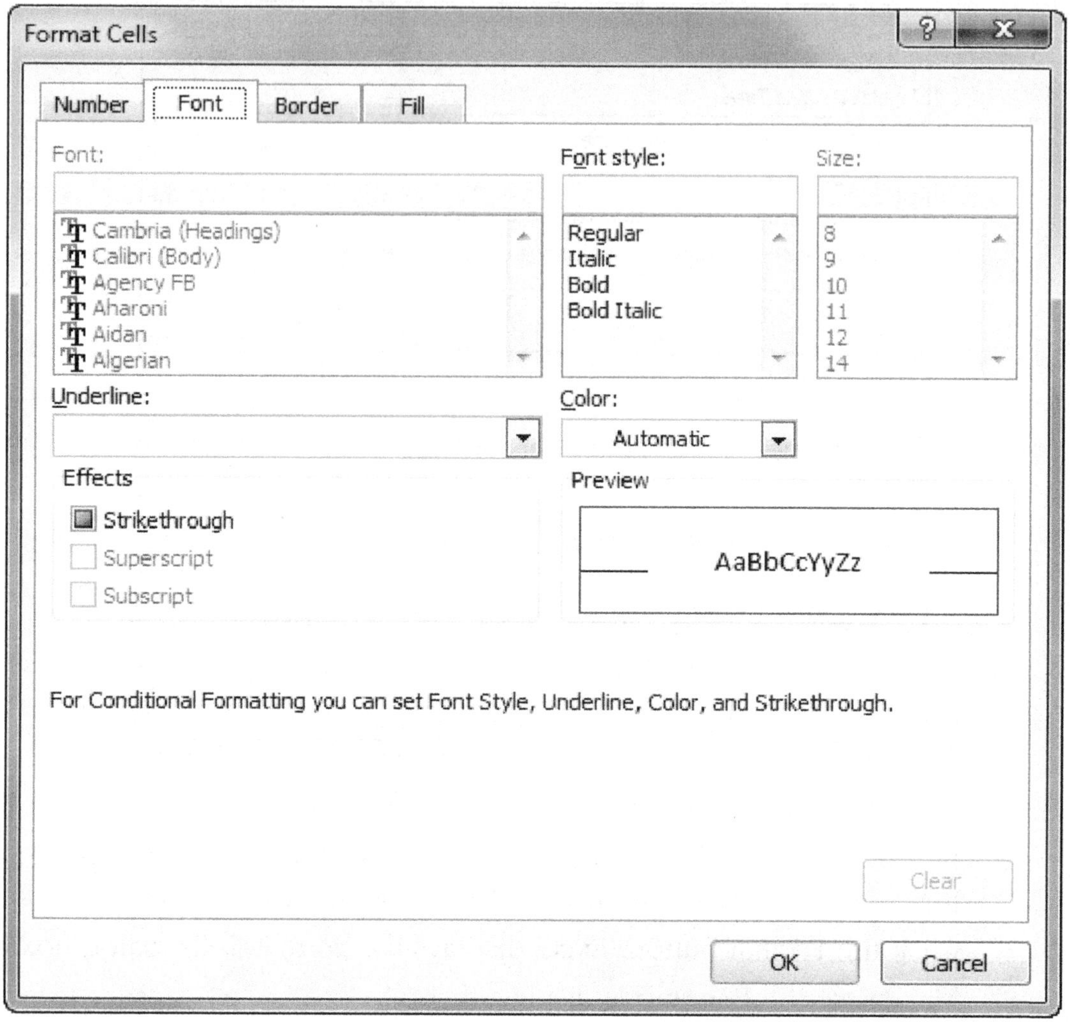

The Font tab of the Format Cells dialog box.

9. Use the Color drop-down list to choose white.
10. Click OK to dismiss the Format Cells dialog box.
11. Click OK to dismiss the New Formatting Rule dialog box.
12. Print your worksheet as normal. The cell contents should not show up on the printout.
13. To make the cell contents visible on the printout, just modify cell J1 so that it contains something other than the letter "p."

Another solution is to use a custom format for the cells whose content you want to hide. Follow these steps:

1. Select the cell (or cells) you want to hide.
2. Display the Home tab of the ribbon.
3. Click the small icon at the lower-right corner of the Number group. Excel displays the Format Cells dialog box.
4. Make sure the Number tab is displayed.

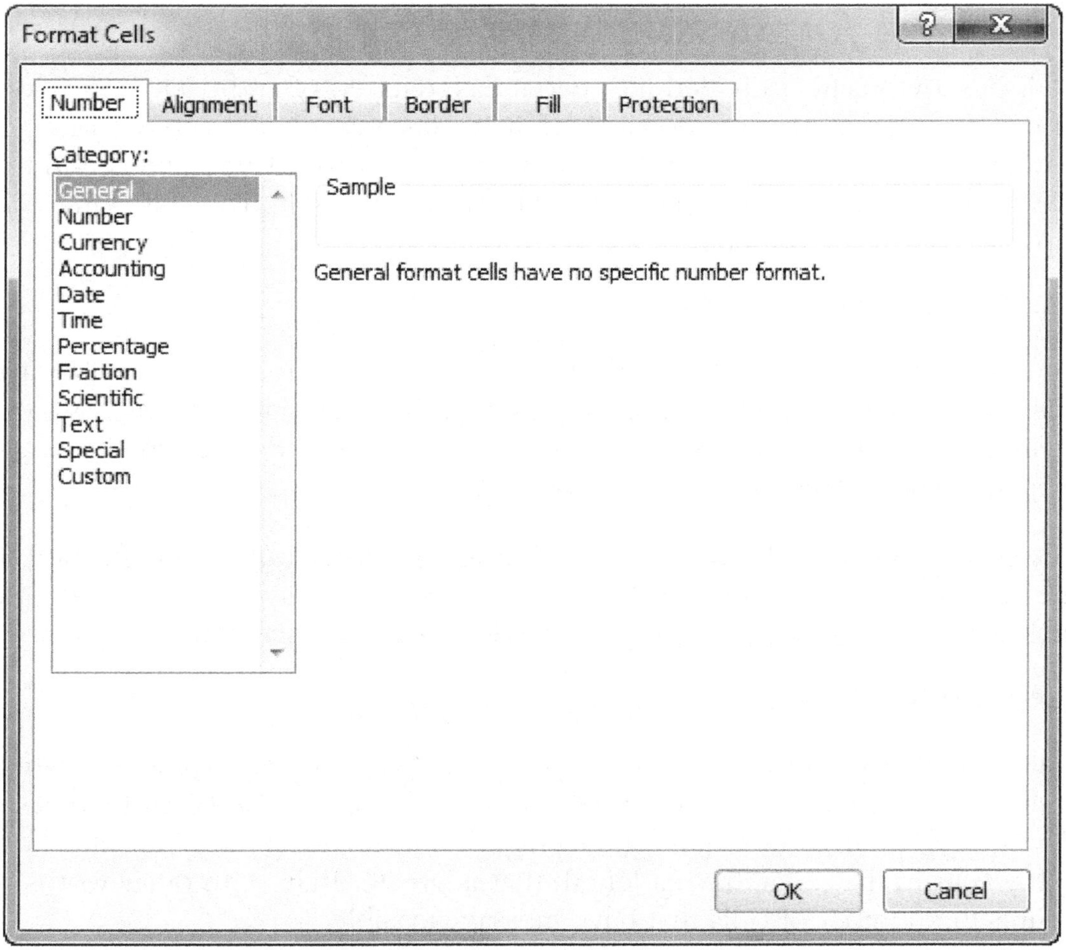

The Number tab of the Format Cells dialog box.

5. In the list of format categories, select Custom.
6. In the Type box, enter three semicolons (;;;).
7. Click on OK.

Now the information in the cell is not visible, nor will it print. You can, however, see the information in the Formula Bar, and it can be overwritten if you enter anything else in the cell.

Checking for Messages in Cells

Blair has a worksheet divided into two areas: data entry and data verification. The data verification area consists of formulas that check entries using IF statements. If a problem is located, a text message is displayed in a cell in the verification area, otherwise the formula returns a blank. The following is a typical verification formula:

```
=IF(A1<>5,"Value in A1 is not 5")
```

The problem is that the data verification area can be quite large, which means it is easy to miss one of the text messages. Blair wondered if there was a way to create a formula that examined the data verification area and returned a single message if there were any other messages in the area.

There are a number of different ways that this problem can be approached. If the data verification area is contiguous, then a simple array formula will do the trick. Enter the following in any empty cell on the worksheet:

```
=SUM((LEN(ValRange)>0)*1)
```

Make sure that ValRange is replaced with the range of cells in the data validation area. Also, make sure you enter the formula by pressing **SHIFT+CTRL+ENTER** (to denote it is an array formula). The formula returns a value that indicates how many cells in the range have a length that is greater than 0. In other words, it counts the number of cells that have messages visible.

If you prefer to not use an array formula, you can accomplish the same result by using the following regular formula:

```
=SUMPRODUCT((LEN(ValRange)>0)*1)
```

The result, again, is the number of cells that have a length greater than 0. Another approach is to use some of the COUNT functions provided by Excel:

```
=COUNTA(ValRange) - COUNTBLANK(ValRange)
```

This formula counts the number of cells in the range, and then subtracts the number of blank cells in the range. The result is the number of cells that are non-blank, or those that are displaying messages. A different formulaic approach can be used to determine a simple yes/no response:

```
=IF(COUNTIF(ValRange,"?*"),"","No ") & "Verification Messages"
```

If there are no messages in the ValRange, the formula returns "No Verification Messages." If there are messages, it strips the "No" and simply returns "Verification Messages."

It would also be a good idea to apply conditional formatting to your data verification area. While the formulas discussed so far will tell you if there are messages, it won't highlight where those messages are—conditional formatting can pinpoint each message. Select all the cells in the area that contain formulas, and then use conditional formatting to check the length of those cells. If the length is greater than 0, the cell could be formatted to show a red background. This will make any messages in the data verification area much harder to miss when scrolling through the worksheet.

If you are in the mood to completely redesign your worksheet, a more powerful approach would be to do away with the data verification area. You can achieve the same results (checking what is in the data entry area) by using data validation for each of the entry cells. Set up properly, data validation would make sure that the user entered acceptable values into each cell, removing the need for much of the data validation area.

3

Conditionally Formatting Rows

Conditionally Formatting an Entire Row

Graham described a problem he was having with a worksheet. He wanted to use conditional formatting to highlight all the cells in a row, if the value in column E was greater than a particular value. He was having problems coming up with the proper way to do that.

Suppose for a moment that your data is in cells A3:H50. You can apply the proper conditional formatting by following these steps:

1. Select cell A3.
2. With A3 still selected, scroll the worksheet so you can see cell H50.
3. Hold down the **SHIFT** key as you click on H50. The entire range A3:H50 should be selected, and A3 should still be the active cell.
4. Make sure the Home tab of the ribbon is displayed.
5. Click the Conditional Formatting tool. Excel displays a series of choices.
6. Click New Rule. Excel displays the New Formatting Rule dialog box.
7. In the Select a Rule Type area at the top of the dialog box, choose Use a Formula to Determine Which Cells to Format.

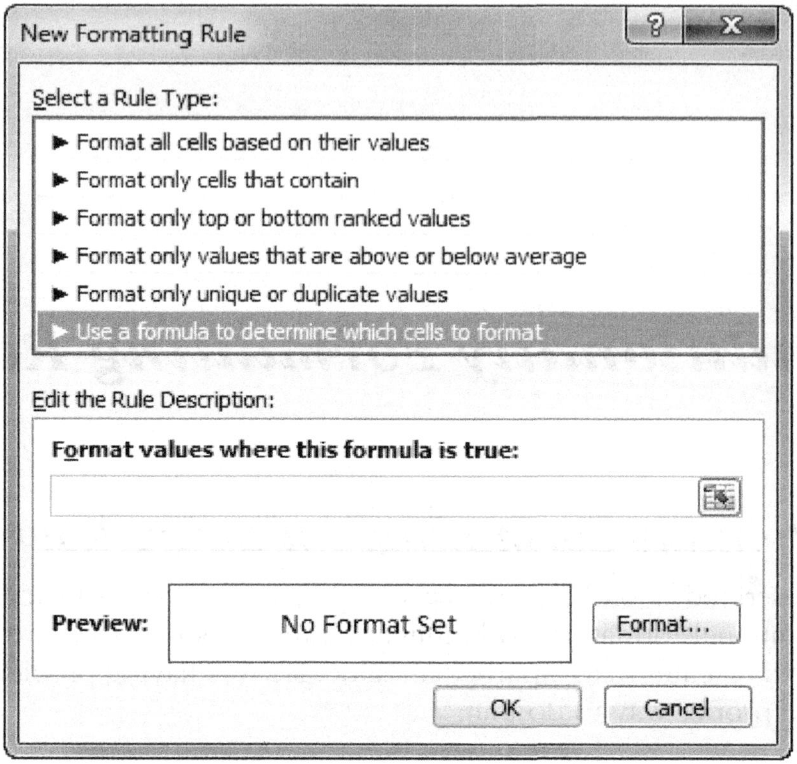

The New Formatting Rule dialog box.

8. In the formula space, enter the following formula:

```
=$E3>40000
```

9. Click the Format button. Excel displays the Format Cells dialog box.

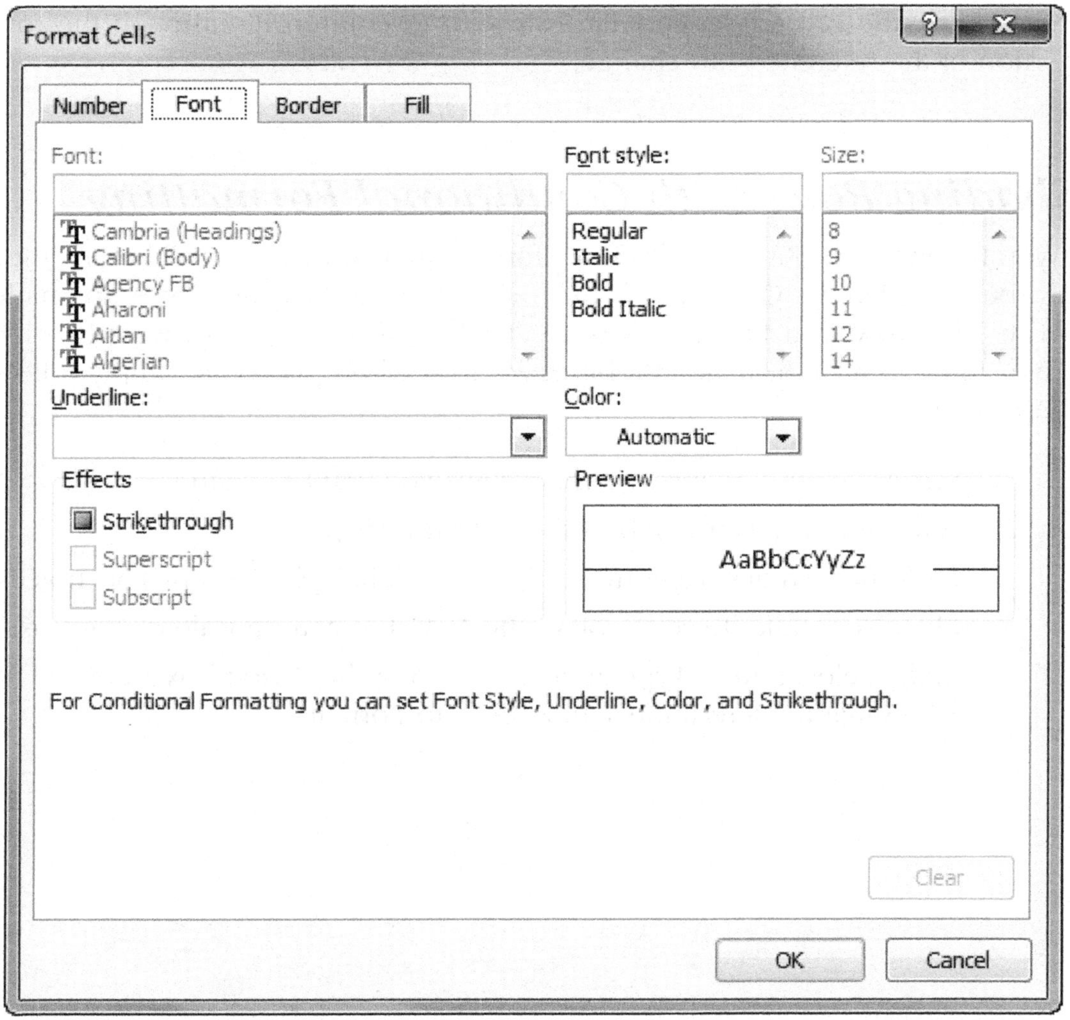

The Format Cells dialog box.

10. Using the controls in the dialog box, specify how you want the cells that are greater than 40,000 to be displayed.
11. Click OK to dismiss the Format Cells dialog box.
12. Click OK to accept your conditional format.

This formula used in the conditional format works because you use the absolute indicator (the dollar sign) just before the column letter. Any reference that has the $ before it is not changed when Excel propagates it throughout a range.

In this case, the cell reference will always be to column E, although the row portion of the reference can change.

Shading Rows with Conditional Formatting

If you haven't tried out the conditional formatting features of Excel before, they can be quite handy. One way to use this feature is to cause Excel to shade every other row in a table. This is great when you have a particularly wide table, and you want to make it a bit easier to read on printouts. Simply follow these steps:

1. Select the table whose alternate rows you want to shade.
2. Make sure the Home tab of the ribbon is displayed.
3. Click the Conditional Formatting tool. Excel displays a series of choices.
4. Click New Rule. Excel displays the New Formatting Rule dialog box.
5. In the Select a Rule Type area at the top of the dialog box, choose Use a Formula to Determine Which Cells to Format.

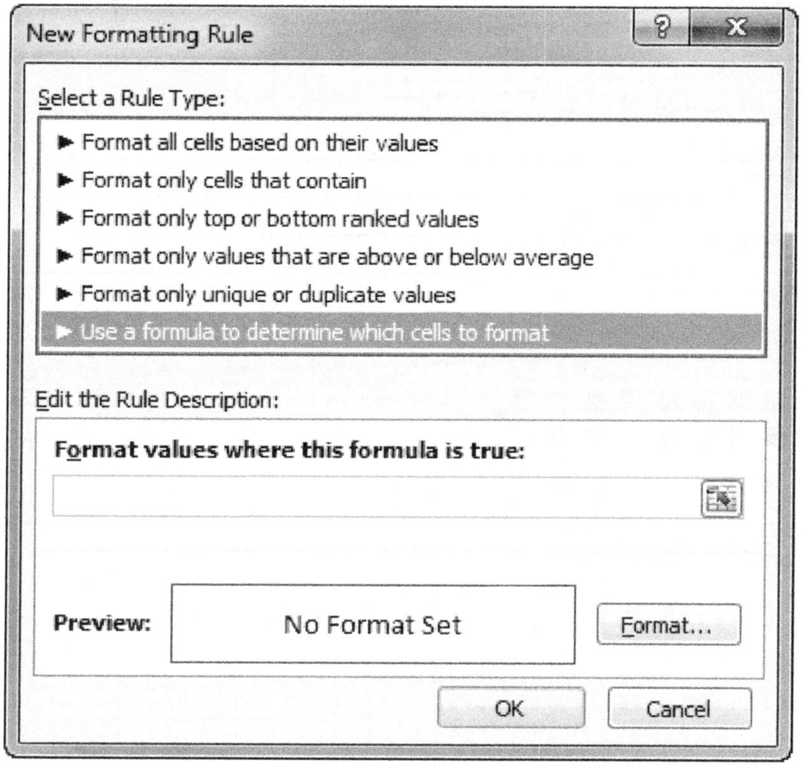

The New Formatting Rule dialog box.

6. In the formula space, enter the following formula:

```
=MOD(ROW(),2)=0
```

7. Click on the Format button. Excel displays the Format Cells dialog box.
8. Make sure the Fill tab is selected.

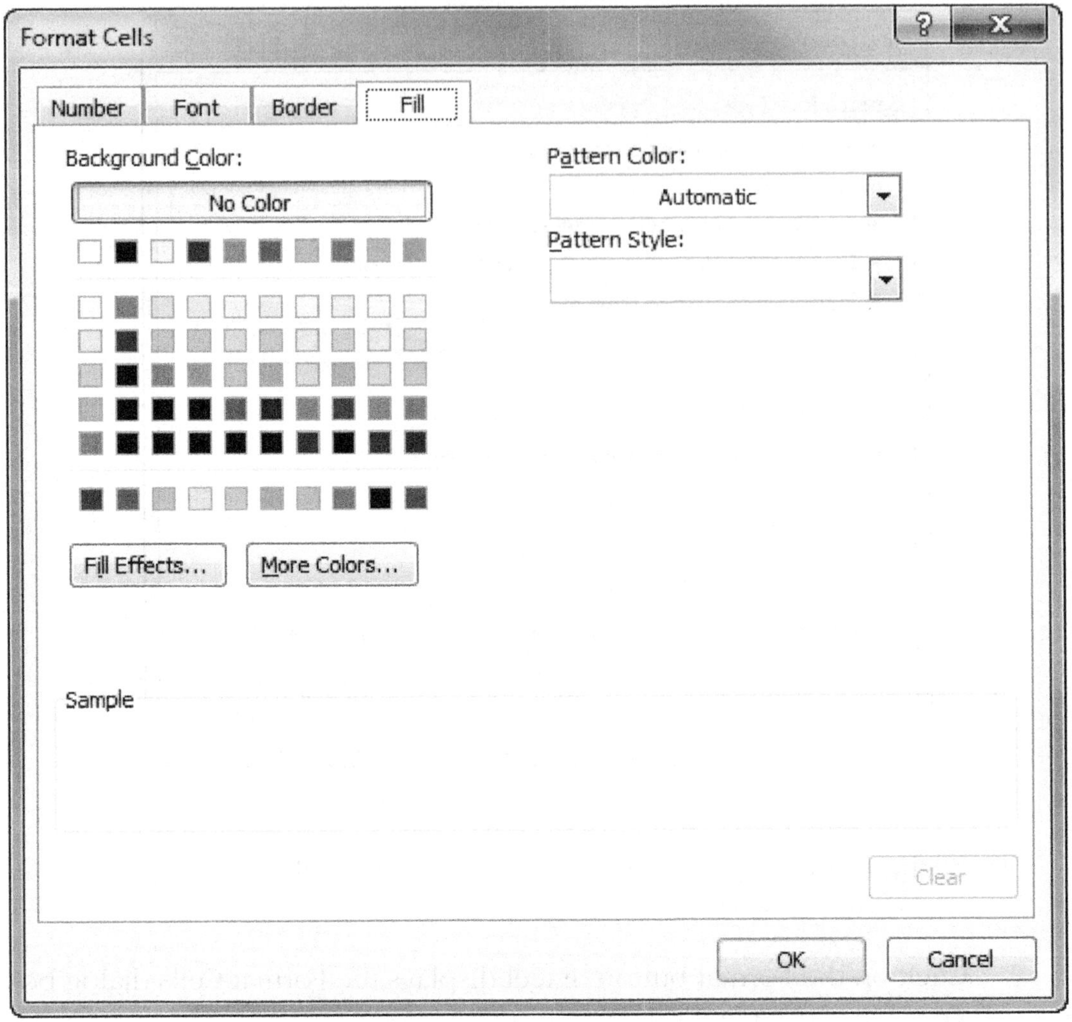

The Fill tab of the Format Cells dialog box.

9. Select the color you want used for the row shading.
10. Click on OK to close the Format Cells dialog box.
11. Click on OK to close the New Formatting Rule dialog box.

Those familiar with Excel may wonder why anyone would use conditional formatting to highlight different rows of a table when you can use the table formatting feature (available in the Styles group of the Home tab of the ribbon) to accomplish the same thing. The reason is simple—using conditional formatting provides much more flexibility in the formatting applied as well as in the interval of the rows being shaded.

Automatic Lines for Dividing Lists

Let's say you have a list of company transactions. Each transaction includes a department number, a title, and other information (amount, date, time, sales rep, etc.). As you get more and more of these items in your list, you may want a way to automatically add "dividing lines" based on the department number. For instance, when the department number changes, you may want to include a line between the two departments.

To add this type of formatting to your list, start by sorting your data table by department. Then follow these steps:

1. Select the left-most cell of the first row of your data. For instance, if your table heads are in row 3 (columns A through J), and your first row of data is in row 4, you should select cell A4.
2. Press **Shift+Ctrl+End**. All the cells in your data table should be selected, with the exception of the header row.
3. With the Home tab of the ruler displayed, click the Conditional Formatting option in the Styles group. Excel displays a palette of options related to conditional formatting.
4. Click New Rule. Excel displays the New Formatting Rule dialog box.
5. In the Select a Rule Type area at the top of the dialog box, choose Use a Formula to Determine Which Cells to Format.

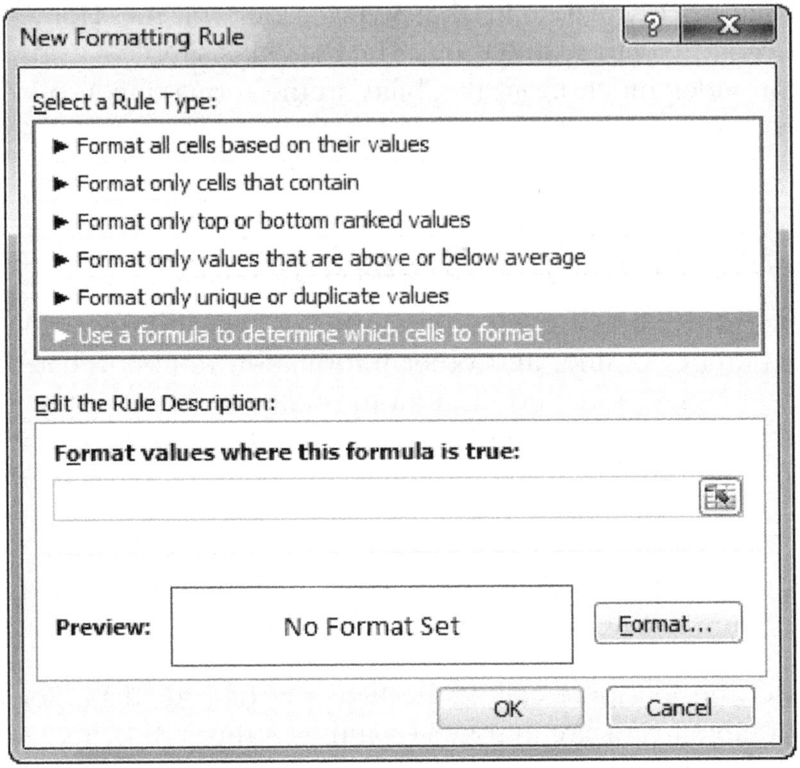

The New Formatting Rule dialog box.

6. In the Format Values Where This Formula Is True box, enter "=$A4<>$A5" (without the quote marks).
7. Click Format to display the Format Cells dialog box.
8. Display the Border tab.
9. Click the None button to remove any borders already applied to the cells.
10. In the Style list, select the type of border you want to appear between departments.
11. In the Border area of the dialog box, click the button that adds your selected border style to the bottom of the cells.

12. Click OK to dismiss the Format Cells dialog box. The formatting you specified in steps 10 and 11 should now appear in the preview area for the rule.
13. Click OK.

That's it; you should now see a line that appears across the entire width of your data every time the department changes.

Formatting Subtotal Rows

When you add subtotals to a worksheet, Excel automatically formats the subtotals using a bold font. You, however, may want to have some different type of formatting for the subtotals, such as shading them in yellow or a different color.

If you use subtotals sparingly, and only want to apply a different format for one or two worksheets, you can follow these general steps:

1. Apply your subtotals, as desired.
2. Select the entire data table, including the subtotals.
3. Using the Outline area at the left of the screen, collapse the detail in your worksheet so that only the subtotals are showing.
4. Press **F5** to display the Go To dialog box.

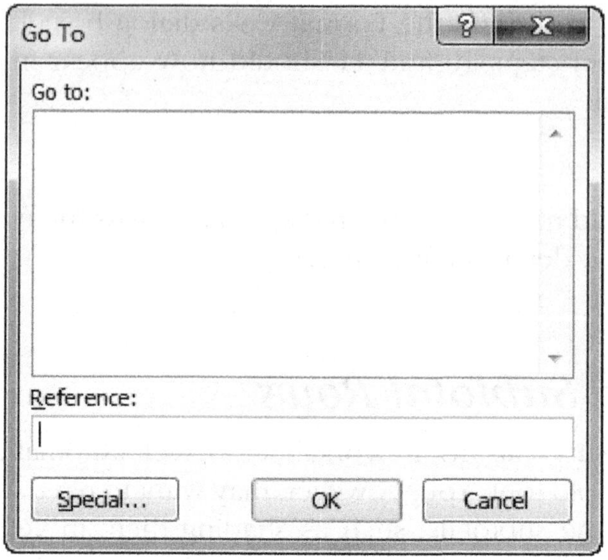

The Go To dialog box.

5. Click Special to display the Go To Special dialog box.

The Go To Special dialog box.

6. Select the Visible Cells Only option button.
7. Click OK. Now, only the visible subtotal rows are selected.
8. Apply your formatting, as desired.

If you will be repeatedly adding and removing subtotals to the same data table, you may be interested in using conditional formatting to apply the desired subtotal formatting. Follow these steps:

1. Before applying your subtotals, select your entire data table.
2. Make sure the Home tab of the ribbon is displayed.
3. Click the Conditional Formatting tool. Excel displays a series of choices.
4. Click Manage Rules. Excel displays the Conditional Formatting Rules Manager dialog box.
5. Click New Rule. Excel displays the New Formatting Rule dialog box.
6. In the Select a Rule Type area at the top of the dialog box, choose Use a Formula to Determine Which Cells to Format.

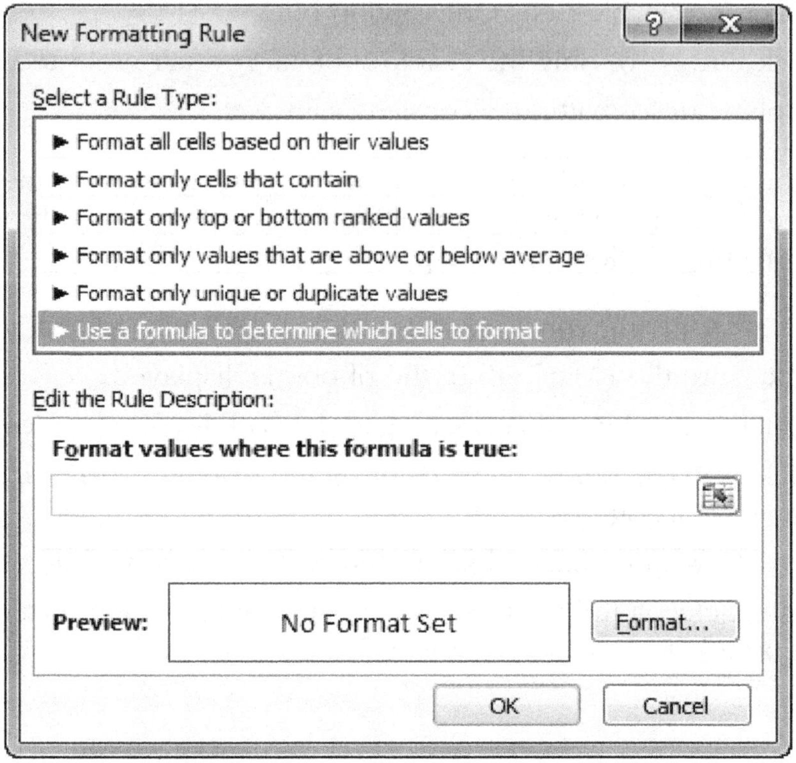

The New Formatting Rule dialog box.

7. In the formula space, enter the following formula:

```
=ISNUMBER(FIND("Grand Total",$A1))
```

8. Click Format to display the Format Cells dialog box.
9. Using the controls in the dialog box, set the formatting as you want it applied to the Grand Total row.
10. Click OK to dismiss the Format Cells dialog box.
11. Click OK to dismiss the New Formatting Rule dialog box. The rule you just created now appears in the Conditional Formatting Rules Manager dialog box.
12. Click New Rule. Excel again displays the New Formatting Rule dialog box.
13. In the Select a Rule Type area at the top of the dialog box, choose Use a Formula to Determine Which Cells to Format.

14. In the formula box, enter the following formula:

```
=ISNUMBER(FIND("Total",$A1))
```

15. Click Format to display the Format Cells dialog box.

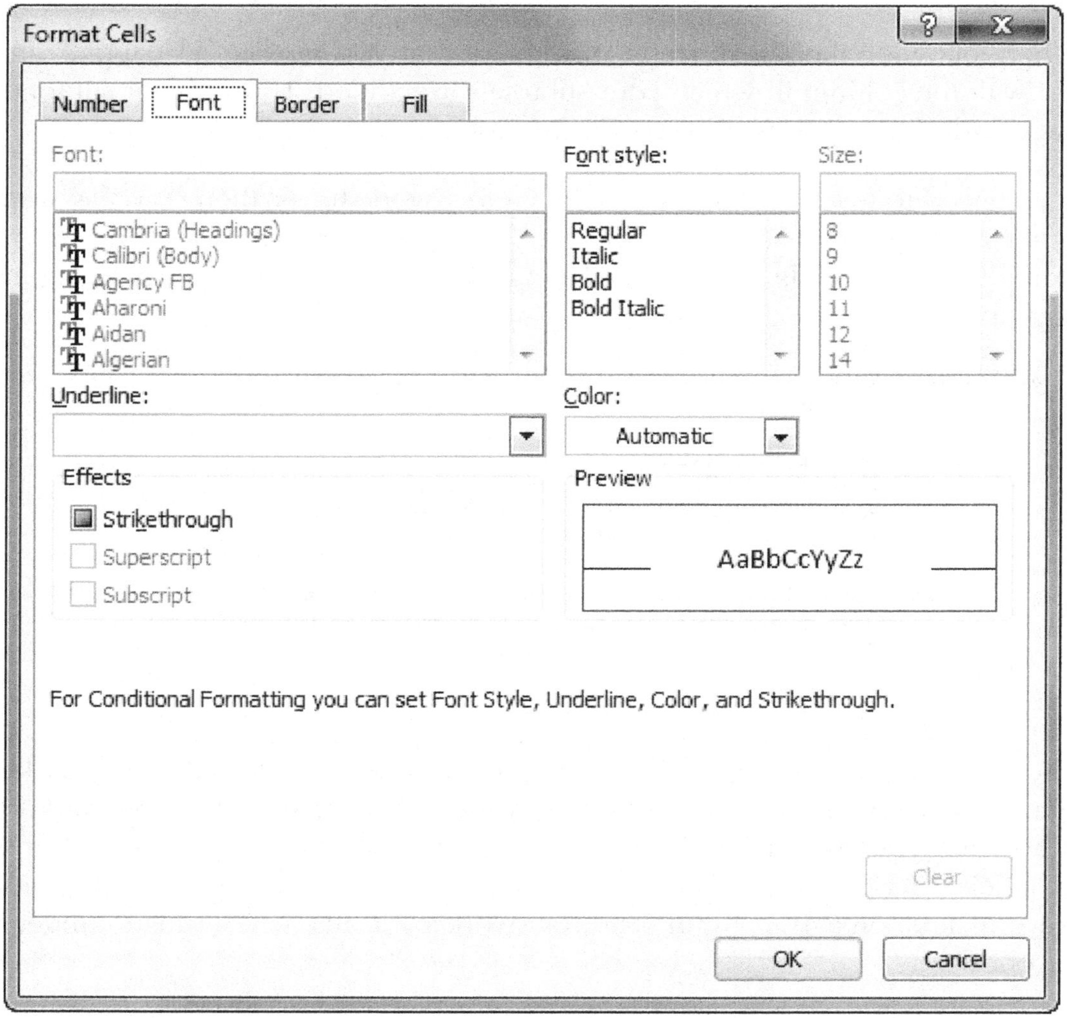

The Format Cells dialog box.

16. Using the controls in the dialog box, set the formatting as you want it applied to the Total row.
17. Click OK to dismiss the Format Cells dialog box.

18. Click OK to dismiss the New Formatting Rule dialog box.
19. Click the up and down arrows to move the rules you created to the order in which they should be evaluated.
20. Click OK to dismiss the Conditional Formatting Rules Manager dialog box.

When following the above steps, make sure that you replace A1 (steps 7 and 14) with the column in which your subtotals are added. Thus, if your subtotals are in column G, you would use G1 instead of A1.

If you need to format subtotals on quite a few worksheets, then you may want to create a macro that will do the formatting for you. The following macro examines all the cells in a selected range, and then applies cell coloring, as appropriate.

```
Sub FormatTotalRows()
    Dim rCell as Range

    For Each rCell In Selection
        If Right(rCell.Value, 5) = "Total" Then
            Rows(rCell.Row).Interior.ColorIndex = 36
        End If

        If Right(rCell.Value, 11) = "Grand Total" Then
            Rows(rCell.Row).Interior.ColorIndex = 44
        End If
    Next
End Sub
```

The macro colors the subtotal rows yellow and the grand total row a darker shade of yellow. (The exact colors on your system may vary depending on the theme you have loaded.) The macro, although simple in nature, is not as efficient as it could be since every cell in the selected range is inspected. Nevertheless, on a 10 column 5000 row worksheet this macro runs in under 5 seconds.

4

Real-World Conditional Formatting

Alerts for Approaching Due Dates

Jonathan developed a worksheet that tracks due dates for various departmental documents. He wondered if there was a way for Excel to somehow alert him if the due date for a particular document was approaching.

There are several ways that this can be done in Excel, and you should pick the method that is best for your purposes. The first method is to simply add a column to your worksheet that will be used for the alert. Assuming your due date is in column F, you could place the following type of formula in column G:

```
=IF(F3<(TODAY()+7),"<<<","")
```

The formula checks to see if the date in cell F3 is earlier than a week from today. If so, then the formula displays "<<<" in the cell. The effect of this formula is to alert you to any date that is either past or within the next week.

Another approach is to use the conditional formatting capabilities of Excel. Follow these steps:

1. Select the cells that contain the document due dates.
2. Make sure the Home tab of the ribbon is displayed.

3. Click the Conditional Formatting option in the Styles group. On the resulting submenu, click Manage Rules. Excel displays the Conditional Formatting Rules Manager dialog box.

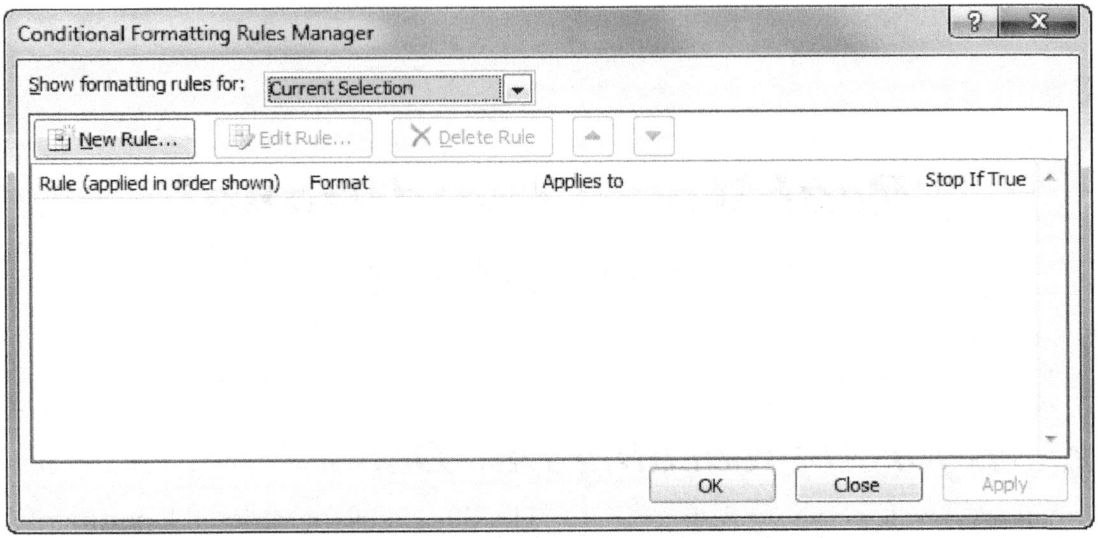

The Conditional Formatting Rules Manager dialog box.

4. Click the New Rule button. Excel displays the New Formatting Rule dialog box.
5. In the Select a Rule Type list, choose Format Only Cells That Contain.

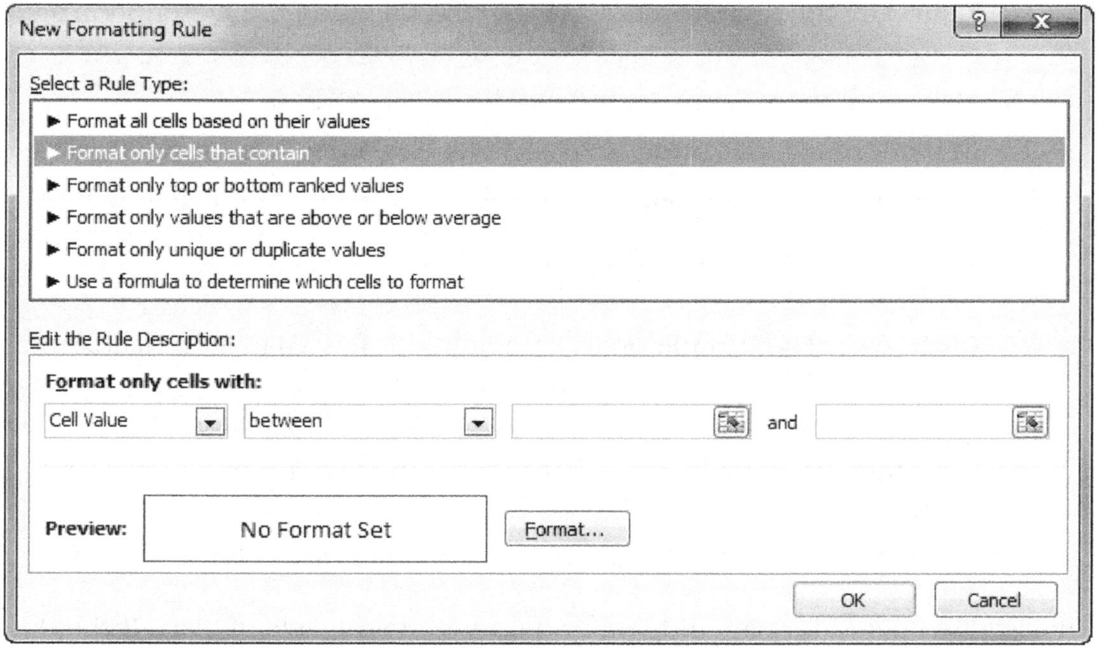

The New Formatting Rule dialog box.

6. Make sure the first drop-down list in the Edit the Rule Description area is "Cell Value." (This should be the default.)
7. Make sure the second drop-down list is "Less Than."
8. In the formula area, enter "=TODAY()" (without the quote marks).
9. Click the Format button. Excel displays the Format Cells dialog box.
10. Using the Color drop-down list, choose the color red.
11. Click OK to close the Format Cells dialog box.
12. Click OK. The Conditional Formatting Rules Manager dialog box reappears with your newly defined condition in it.
13. Click the New Rule button. Excel displays the New Formatting Rule dialog box.
14. In the Select a Rule Type List, choose Format Only Cells That Contain.

15. Make sure the first drop-down list in the Edit the Rule Description area is "Cell Value." (This should be the default.)
16. Make sure the second drop-down list is "Less Than."
17. In the formula area, enter "=TODAY()+7" (without the quote marks).
18. Click the Format button. Excel displays the Format Cells dialog box.
19. Using the Color drop-down list, choose the color blue.
20. Click OK to close the Format Cells dialog box.
21. Click OK. The Conditional Formatting Rules Manager dialog box reappears with your newly defined condition in it. (The newly defined condition should actually be selected in the list of conditions.)
22. Click the Move Down arrow. This moves the last condition you defined (steps 13 through 21) so it is in the proper order.
23. Click OK to close the Conditional Formatting dialog box.

This is a two-tiered format, and you end up with two levels of alert. If the due date is already past, then it shows up as red. If the due date is today or within the next seven days, then it shows up in blue.

Pulling All Fridays

When developing a worksheet to track business information, you may have a need to determine all the Fridays in a range of dates. The best way to do this depends on the data in your worksheet and the way in which you want results displayed.

If you have a list of dates in a column, you can use several different worksheet functions to determine whether those dates are Fridays or not. The WEEKDAY function returns a number, 1 through 7, depending on the weekday of the date used as an argument:

```
=WEEKDAY(A2)
```

This usage returns the number 6 if the date in A2 is a Friday. If this formula is copied down next to a column of dates, you could then use the AutoFilter feature of Excel to show only those dates where the weekday is 6 (Friday).

You could also use the conditional formatting feature of Excel to simply highlight all the Fridays in a list of dates. Follow these steps:

1. Select the list of dates.
2. Make sure the Home tab of the ribbon is displayed.
3. Click the Conditional Formatting tool. Excel displays a series of choices.
4. Click New Rule. Excel displays the New Formatting Rule dialog box.
5. In the Select a Rule Type area at the top of the dialog box, choose Use a Formula to Determine Which Cells to Format.

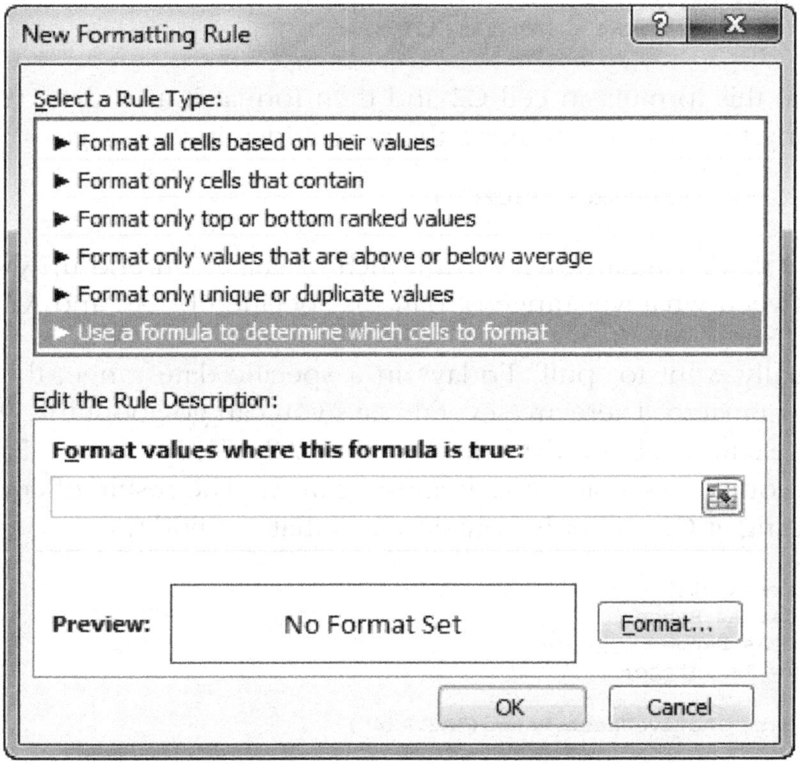

The New Formatting Rule dialog box.

6. In the formula area enter the following formula, replacing A2 with the address of the active cell selected in step 1:

```
=WEEKDAY(A2)=6
```

7. Click Format to display the Format Cells dialog box.
8. Set the formatting options to highlight the Fridays as desired.
9. Click OK to dismiss the Format Cells dialog box.
10. Click OK.

If you want to determine a series of Fridays based on a beginning and ending date, you can set up a series of formulas to figure them out. Assuming that the beginning date is in A2 and the ending date is in A3, you can use the following formula to figure out the date of the first Friday:

```
=IF(A2+IF(WEEKDAY(A2)<=6,6-WEEKDAY(A2),6)>A3,
"",A2+IF(WEEKDAY(A2)<=6,6-WEEKDAY(A2),6))
```

If you place this formula in cell C2 and then format it as a date, you can use the following formula to determine the next Friday in the range:

```
=IF(C2="","",IF(C2+7>$A$3,"",C2+7))
```

If you copy this formula down for a bunch of cells, you end up with a list of Fridays between whatever range of dates is specified by A2 and A3.

If you actually want to "pull" Fridays in a specific date range, then you will need to use a macro. There are several ways you can go about this. This simple macro will examine all the dates in the range A2:A24. If they are Fridays, then the date is copied into column C, beginning at C2. The result, of course, is that the list starting at C2 will only contain dates that are Fridays.

```
Sub PullFridays1()
    Dim dat As Range
    Dim c As Range
    Dim rw As Integer

    Set dat = ActiveSheet.Range("A2:A24")
    rw = 2
    For Each c In dat
        If Weekday(c) = vbFriday Then
            Cells(rw, 3).Value = Format(c)
            rw = rw + 1
        End If
    Next
End Sub
```

If desired, you can change the range examined by the macro simply by changing the A2:A24 reference, and you can change where the dates are written by changing the value of rw (the row) and the value 3 (the column) in the Cells function.

If you would rather work with a beginning date and an ending date, you can modify the macro so that it will step through the dates. The following macro assumes that the beginning date is in cell A2 and the ending date is in cell A3.

```
Sub PullFridays2()
    Dim dStart As Date
    Dim dEnd As Date
    Dim rw As Integer

    dStart = Range("A2").Value
    dEnd = Range("A3").Value

    rw = 2
    While dStart < dEnd
        If Weekday(dStart) = vbFriday Then
            Cells(rw, 3).Value = dStart
            Cells(rw, 3).NumberFormat = "m/d/yyyy"
            rw = rw + 1
        End If
        dStart = dStart + 1
    Wend
End Sub
```

The macro still pulls the Fridays from the range and places them into a list starting at C2.

Another macro approach is to create a user-defined function that returns specific Fridays within a range. The following does just that:

```
Function PullFridays3(dStartDate As Date, _
                      dEndDate As Date, _
                      iIndex As Integer)
    Dim iMaxDays As Integer
    Dim dFirstday As Date

    Application.Volatile
    If dStartDate > dEndDate Then
        PullFridays3 = CVErr(xlErrNum)
        Exit Function
    End If
```

```
        dFirstday = vbFriday - Weekday(dStartDate) + dStartDate
        If dFirstday < dStartDate Then dFirstday = dFirstday + 7
        iMaxDays = Int((dEndDate - dFirstday) / 7) + 1

        PullFridays3 = ""
        If iIndex = 0 Then
            PullFridays3 = iMaxDays
        ElseIf iIndex <= iMaxDays Then
            PullFridays3 = dFirstday + (iIndex - 1) * 7
        End If
    End Function
```

You use this function in a cell in your worksheet in the following manner:

```
=PULLFRIDAYS3(A2,A3,1)
```

The first argument for the function is the starting date and the second is the ending date. The third argument indicates which Friday you want returned from within the specified range. If you use 1, you get the first Friday, 2 returns the second Friday, etc. If you use a 0 for the third argument, then the function returns the number of Fridays in the specified range. If the specified beginning date is greater than the ending date, then the function returns a #NUM error.

Conditional Formatting Based on Date Proximity

Richard wondered if it was possible, using conditional formatting, to change the color of a cell. For his purposes he wanted a cell to be red if it contains today's date, to be yellow if it contains a date within a week of today, and to be green if it contains a date within two weeks.

You can achieve this type of conditional formatting if you apply a formula. For instance, let's assume that you want to apply the conditional formatting to cell A1. Just follow these steps:

1. Select cell A1.
2. With the Home tab of the ribbon displayed, click the Conditional Formatting option in the Styles group. Excel displays a palette of options related to conditional formatting.
3. Choose Manage Rules. Excel displays the Conditional Formatting Rules Manager dialog box.

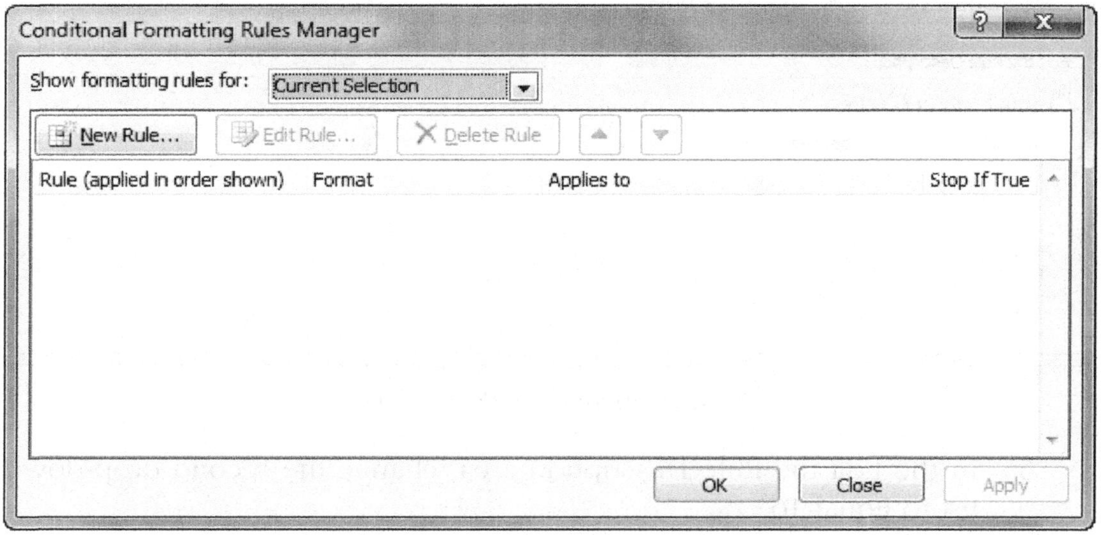

The Conditional Formatting Rules Manager dialog box.

4. Click New Rule. Excel displays the New Formatting Rule dialog box.
5. In the Select a Rule Type area at the top of the dialog box, choose Format Only Cells that Contain.

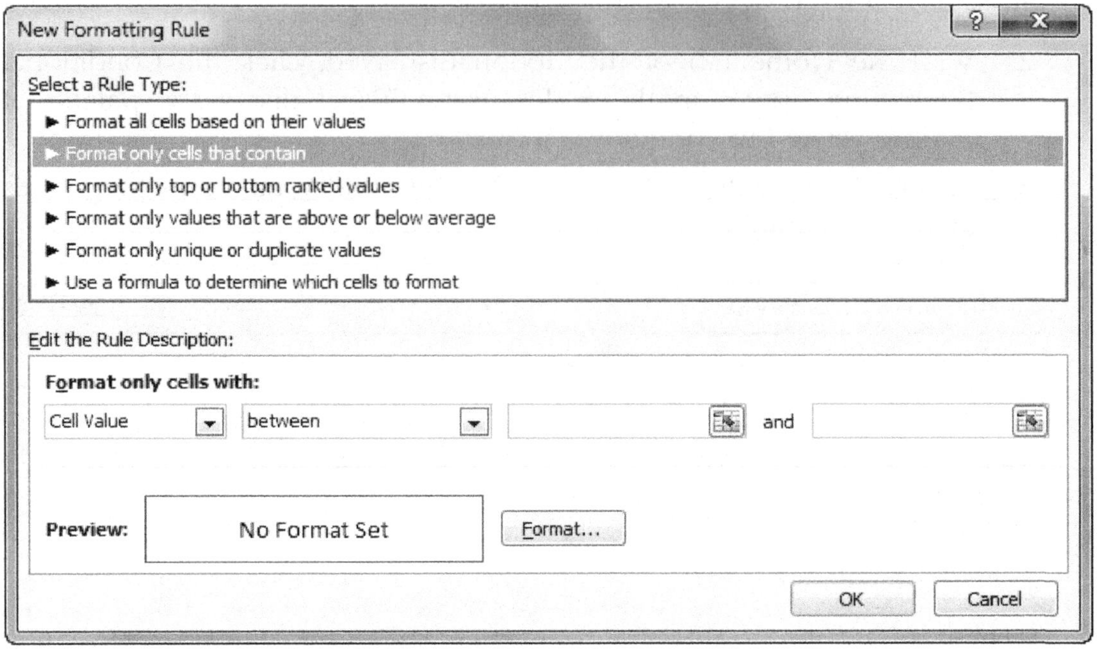

The New Formatting Rule dialog box.

6. In the Edit the Rule Description area, change the second drop-down list to Equal To.
7. In the area just to the right of the drop-down list enter the formula =TODAY(). Note that you must, in the right-most box, enter an equal sign followed by the TODAY() function.
8. Click Format to display the Format Cells dialog box and display the Fill tab.
9. Specify that you want the color of the cell to be red.
10. Click OK to dismiss the Format Cells dialog box. The formatting you specified in step 7 should now appear in the preview area for the rule.
11. Click OK. The New Formatting Rule dialog box disappears and the newly defined rule is shown in the Conditional Formatting Rules Manager dialog box.
12. Click New Rule. Excel again displays the New Formatting Rule dialog box.

13. In the Select a Rule Type area at the top of the dialog box, choose Format Only Cells that Contain.
14. In the Edit the Rule Description area, change the second drop-down list to Between.
15. In the areas just to the right of the drop-down list enter the formulas =TODAY()-7 and =TODAY()+7. Note that you must use equal signs in the two right-most boxes, otherwise Excel can't figure out that you are entering a formula.
16. Click Format to display the Format Cells dialog box and display the Fill tab.
17. Specify that you want the color of the cell to be yellow.
18. Click OK to dismiss the Format Cells dialog box. The formatting you specified in step 7 should now appear in the preview area for the rule.
19. Click OK. The New Formatting Rule dialog box disappears and the newly defined rule is shown in the Conditional Formatting Rules Manager dialog box.
20. Click New Rule. Excel again displays the New Formatting Rule dialog box.
21. In the Select a Rule Type area at the top of the dialog box, choose Format Only Cells that Contain.
22. In the Edit the Rule Description area, change the second drop-down list to Between.
23. In the areas just to the right of the drop-down list enter the formulas =TODAY()-14 and =TODAY()+14. Note that you must use equal signs in the two right-most boxes, otherwise Excel can't figure out that you are entering a formula.
24. Click Format to display the Format Cells dialog box and display the Fill tab.
25. Specify that you want the color of the cell to be green.
26. Click OK to dismiss the Format Cells dialog box. The formatting you specified in step 7 should now appear in the preview area for the rule.

27. Click OK. The New Formatting Rule dialog box disappears and the newly defined rule is shown in the Conditional Formatting Rules Manager dialog box.
28. Use the up and down arrows at the top of the dialog box to put your three rules in the proper order: red, yellow, green.
29. Make sure the Stop If True checkboxes are selected at the right side of each rule.

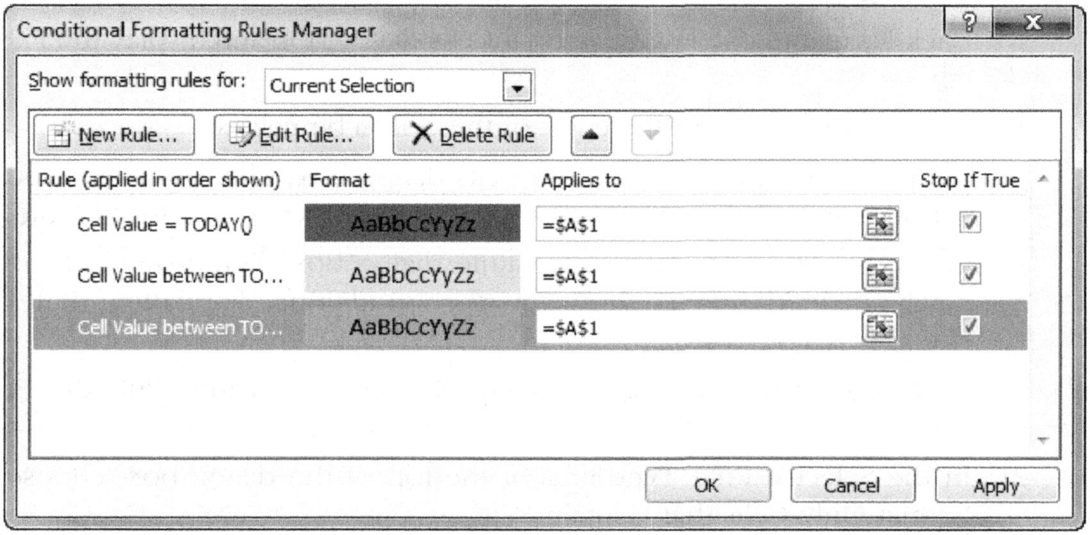

The Conditional Formatting Rules Manager dialog box.

30. Click OK.

One important thing to bear in mind with conditional formatting is that criteria are evaluated in the order in which they appear. Once a criterion has been met, then the formatting is applied and other criteria are not tested. It is therefore important to set out the tests in the correct order. If, in the example above, the criteria had been entered in the reverse order, i.e. test for 14 days, then 7 and then 0, it would have only applied the 14 days format even if the date entered was today. In other words, if the date is today then all three of the tests would have been met so you have to be careful of the order in order to get the result you need.

Another approach to solve the same problem is to use the icon sets available in Excel. These conveniently allow you to assign colored icons (such as red, yellow, and green "traffic lights") to cells based upon the criteria you specify. This could work very well for what Richard desires, providing that Richard wants to "look forward" and display the three colors based on whether the date is today or in the past (red), within the next week (yellow), or further out than that (green).

Again assuming that cell A1 contains the cell for which conditional formatting is to be specified, follow these steps:

1. Select cell A1.
2. With the Home tab of the ribbon displayed, click the Conditional Formatting option in the Styles group. Excel displays a palette of options related to conditional formatting.
3. Click New Rule. Excel displays the New Formatting Rule dialog box.
4. In the Select a Rule Type area at the top of the dialog box, choose Format All Cells Based On Their Values.
5. Using the Format Style drop-down list, choose Icon Sets.
6. Using the Icon Style drop-down list, choose the option that looks like three traffic lights. (This should be the top option available.)

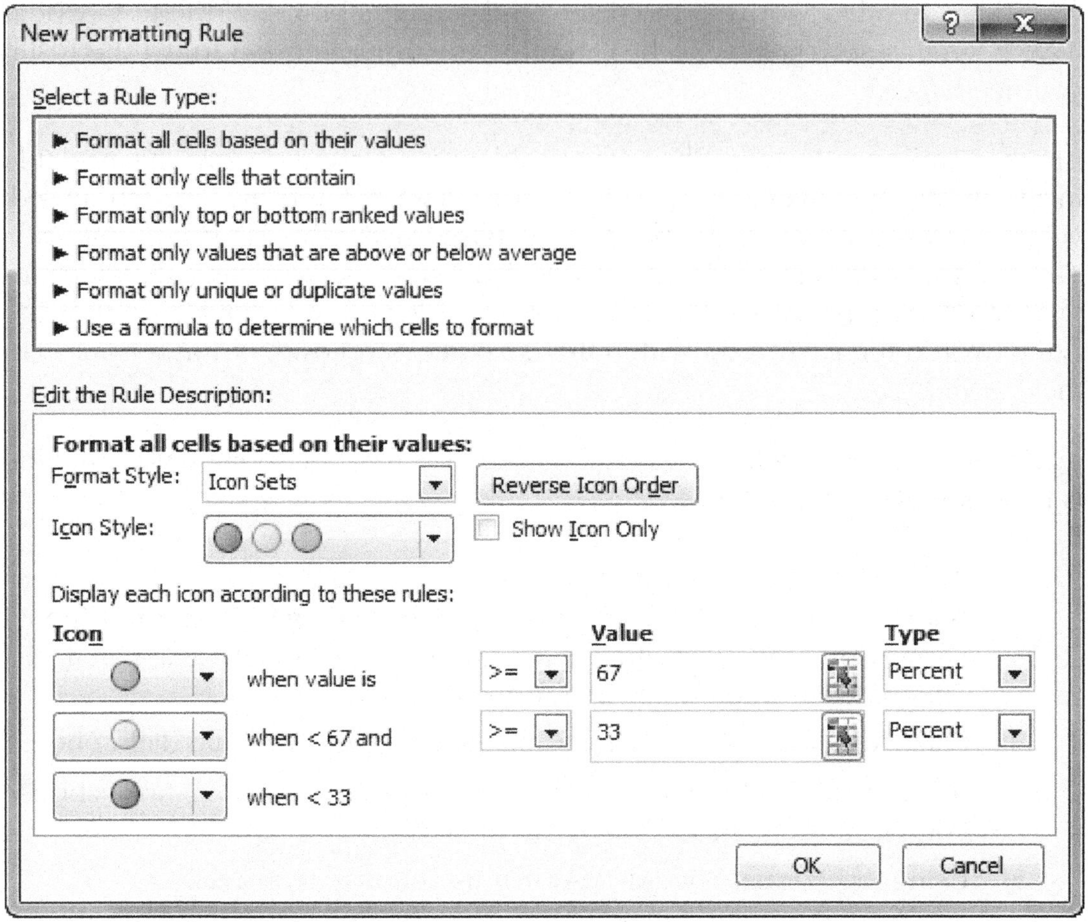

The New Formatting Rule dialog box.

7. Using the Type drop-down lists, choose Formula. (Change both drop-down lists to Formula.)
8. Make sure the operator to the right of the green traffic light is set to >=.
9. In the Value box to the right of the green traffic light, enter the following formula: =TODAY()+8. (This means that the green traffic light will appear for any date beyond a week in the future.)
10. Make sure the operator to the right of the yellow traffic light is set to >.

11. In the Value box to the right of the yellow traffic light, enter the following formula: =TODAY(). (This means that the yellow traffic light will appear for any date greater than today.)
12. Click OK.

Provided your cell width is wide enough, the icon (red, yellow, or green) will appear at the left side of the cell based on the value in the cell.

Conditionally Formatting for Multiple Date Comparisons

Bev is having a problem setting up a conditional format for some cells. What she wants to do is to format the cells so that if they contain a date before today, they will use a bold red font; if they contain a date after today, they will use a bold green font. Bev cannot get both conditions to work properly.

What is probably happening here is a frustrating artifact of the way that Excel parses the conditions you enter. Follow these steps to see what I mean:

1. Select the range of dates to which you want the conditional format applied.
2. With the Home tab of the ribbon displayed, click the Conditional Formatting option in the Styles group. Excel displays a palette of options related to conditional formatting.
3. Choose Manage Rules. Excel displays the Conditional Formatting Rules Manager dialog box.
4. Click New Rule. Excel displays the New Formatting Rule dialog box.
5. In the Select a Rule Type area at the top of the dialog box, choose Format Only Cells that Contain.

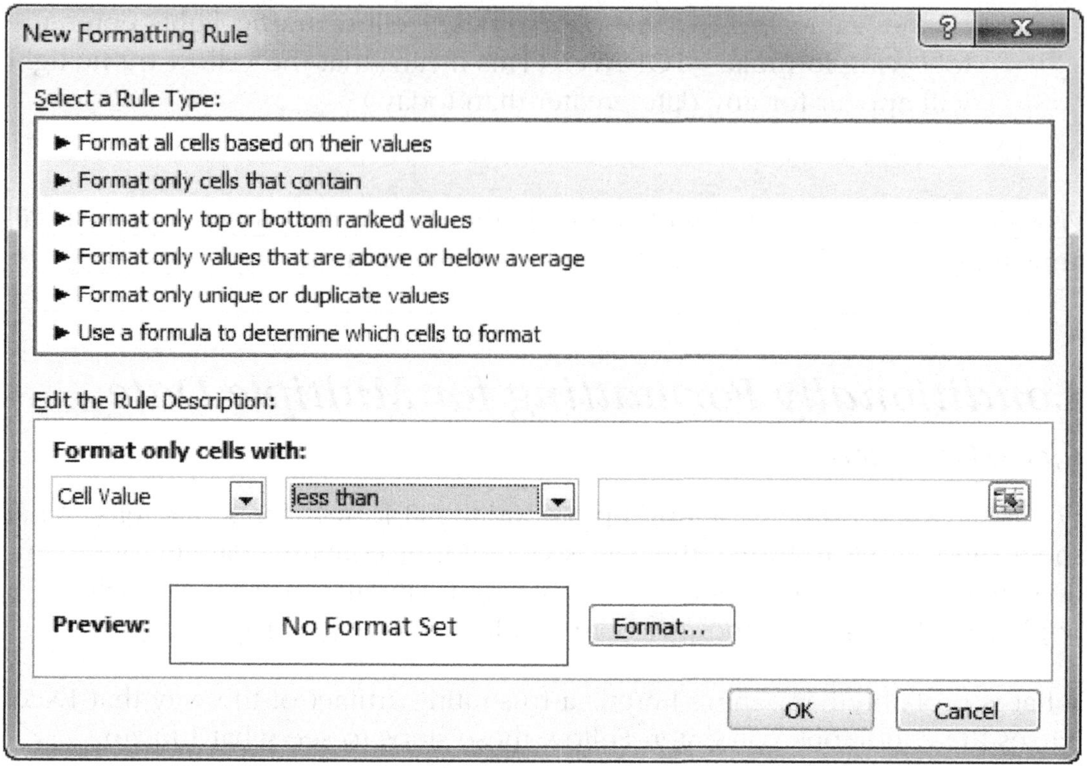

The New Formatting Rule dialog box.

6. In the Edit the Rule Description area, change the second drop-down list to Less Than.
7. In the area just to the right of the drop-down list enter **TODAY()**.
8. Click Format, change the formatting for the font to bold red, then close the Format Cells dialog box.
9. Click OK. Excel closes the New Formatting Rule dialog box and shows the rule in the Conditional Formatting Rules Manager dialog box.
10. Click New Rule. Excel again displays the New Formatting Rule dialog box.
11. In the Select a Rule Type area at the top of the dialog box, choose Format Only Cells that Contain.

12. In the Edit the Rule Description area, change the second drop-down list to Greater Than.
13. In the area just to the right of the drop-down list enter **TODAY()**.
14. Click Format, change the formatting for the font to bold green, then close the Format Cells dialog box.
15. Click OK. Excel closes the New Formatting Rule dialog box and shows the second rule in the Conditional Formatting Rules Manager dialog box.
16. Click the up and down arrows to move the rules you created to the order in which they should be evaluated.
17. Click OK to close the Conditional Formatting Rules Manager dialog box.

At this point there is a very good chance that all the dates in the range are formatted as bold red, even if they are a date after today. This is obviously wrong, and it occurs because of how Excel treats what you entered in the Conditional Formatting or New Formatting Rule dialog boxes. Display each dialog box again (pull up the Conditional Formatting Rules Manager dialog box, select the rule, and click Edit) and examine what you see.

Notice that Excel changed what you entered into the third control for each condition. Instead of appearing as TODAY(), it appears as ="TODAY()". Excel added quotes to what you entered, treating the function name as a string, rather than the actual value for today. Remove the quote marks, but keep the equal sign, then click on OK. The formatting should now be proper; any dates prior to today will be bold red and any after today will be bold green. If the date is today's date, then it will not be formatted in any particular manner.

In the future you can get around the problem by making sure you enter a real formula when creating the conditional rule. You could have done this by adding the equal sign yourself, which designates a formula, in steps 7 and 13 earlier in the tip.

Noting Inactivity within a Timeframe

Graham is a lawyer with several hundred clients. He uses Excel to record time spent on client projects. In column A he notes the client, column B contains the date, column C the start time, and column D the end time. Graham would like to easily identify if he has not done anything for a client for more than three months from the current date.

There are a few ways you can accomplish this task, depending upon the characteristics of the data you are working with. If each client has a single line in the data table then you can use a simple conditional formatting rule to highlight those clients with record dates (column B) older than 90 days. Here's the formula you would use in the rule:

```
=(TODAY()-B2)>=90
```

The formula subtracts the date in B2 from today's date, which provides a number of days between the two dates. If it is greater than or equal to 90, then the formula is true and your conditional format is applied.

This approach can be used if there are multiple records for each client, but it may not provide as clear-cut of an indicator as you might like. If you sort the records by client name, you can easily see which records from each client are over 90 days old. But you would then need to visually make a determination whether all the records for a given client are over 90 days so you can determine if you need to close out their account or not.

It may be better to use a different conditional formatting rule if your data table has multiple records per client. The following formula can be applied to all the clients in column A:

```
=AND(COUNTIF($A$2:$A2,$A2)=COUNTIF($A:$A,$A2),(TODAY()-B2)>=90)
```

It checks to see if there date is outside the desired 90 days, but it only does so if the current record is the last record for the client in the list.

Formatting Phone Numbers outside a Desired Range

If you use Excel to store a list of phone numbers, you may want a way to determine if any of the phone numbers in your list are outside of a specific range. For instance, for your area, only phone numbers in the 240 exchange (those beginning with 240) may be local calls. You might want to highlight all the phone numbers in the list that do not begin with 240, and therefore would be long distance.

The way that you do this depends on whether your phone numbers are stored as text or as formatted numbers. If you enter a phone number with dashes, periods, parentheses, or other non-numeric characters, then the phone number is considered a text entry. If you format the cells as phone numbers (Format Cells dialog box | Number tab | Special | Phone Number), then the phone number is considered a number and formatted for display by Excel.

If your phone numbers are text entries, then use these steps to apply the desired conditional formatting:

1. Select the cells containing the phone numbers. (For the sake of this example, I assume that the first cell you select is A3.)
2. With the Home tab of the ribbon displayed, click the Conditional Formatting option in the Styles group. Excel displays a palette of options related to conditional formatting.
3. Click New Rule. Excel displays the New Formatting Rule dialog box.
4. In the Select a Rule Type area at the top of the dialog box, choose Use a Formula to Determine Which Cells to Format.

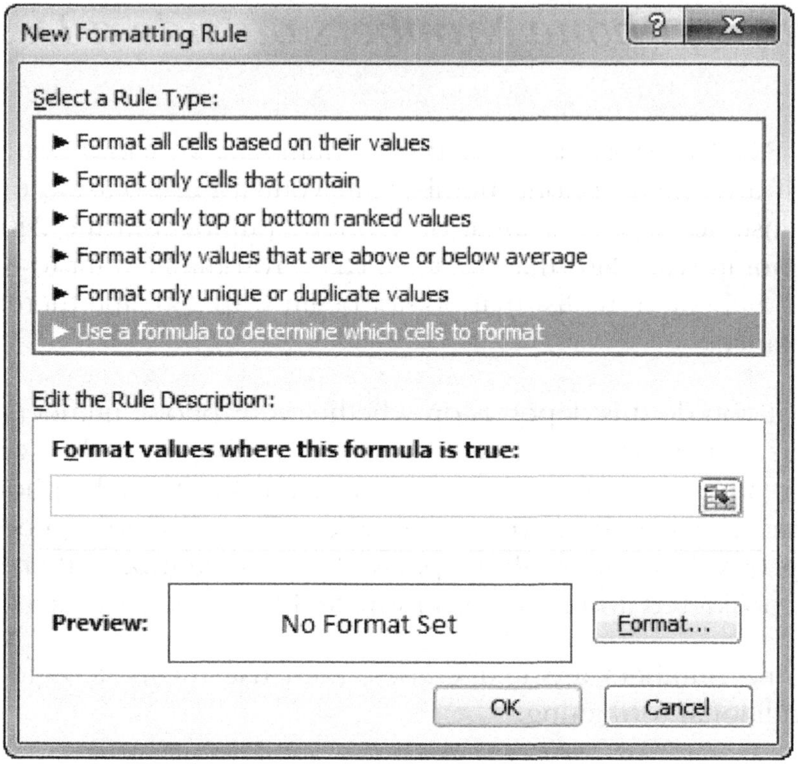

The New Formatting Rule dialog box.

5. In the Format Values Where This Formula Is True box, enter the following formula, replacing A3 with the address of the active cell selected in step 1:

```
=LEFT(A3,3)<>"240"
```

6. Click Format to display the Format Cells dialog box.
7. Set the formatting options to highlight the errant phone numbers, as desired.
8. Click OK to dismiss the Format Cells dialog box. The formatting you specified in step 7 should now appear in the preview area for the rule.
9. Click OK.

These steps will even work if the phone numbers are numeric, but you may want to use a different approach if the phone numbers were entered as numbers. These steps will work:

1. Select the cells containing the phone numbers. (For the sake of this example, I assume that the first cell you select is A3.)
2. With the Home tab of the ruler displayed, click the Conditional Formatting option in the Styles group. Excel displays a palette of options related to conditional formatting.
3. Click New Rule. Excel displays the New Formatting Rule dialog box.
4. In the Select a Rule Type area at the top of the dialog box, choose Format Only Cells That Contain. The left portion of the rule description should automatically be set to Cell Value.
5. Use the next drop-down list in the rule description to choose Not Between.
6. Set the lower and upper boundaries of the condition to 2400000 and 2409999, respectively. (You are specifying that the condition is met if the number is not between 2400000 and 2409999, which is the range of acceptable phone numbers.)

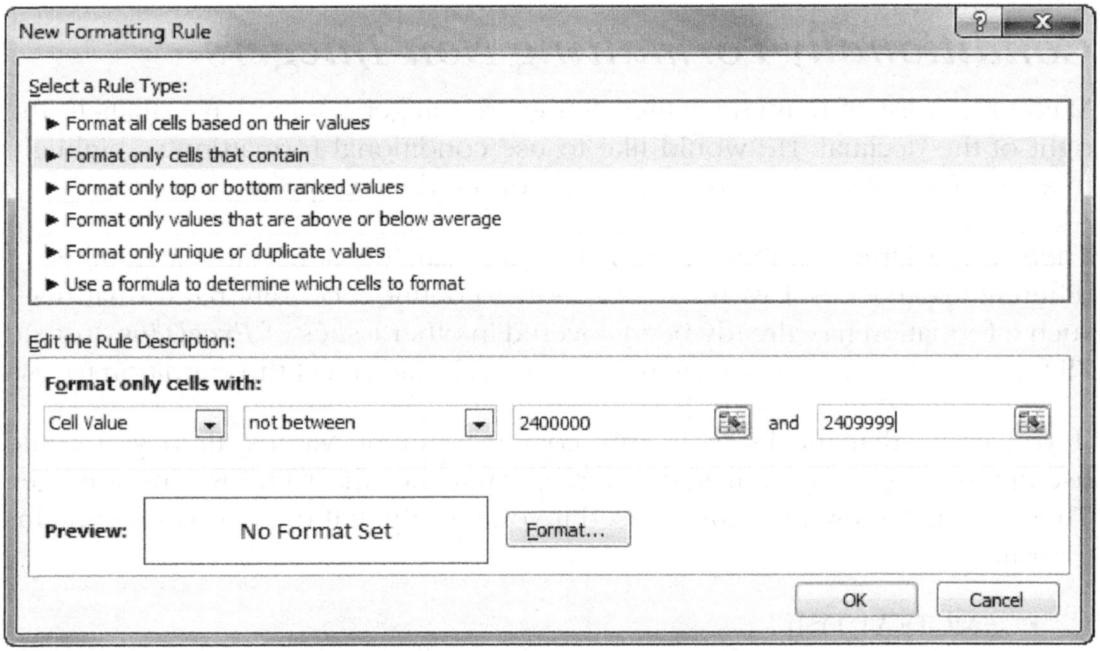

The New Formatting Rule dialog box.

7. Click Format to display the Format Cells dialog box.

8. Set the formatting options to highlight the errant phone numbers, as desired.
9. Click OK to dismiss the Format Cells dialog box. The formatting you specified in step 8 should now appear in the preview area for the condition.
10. Click OK.

If you want to convert your textual phone numbers to numeric phone numbers, so that you can use this last method of conditional formatting, you need to "clean up" your list of numbers. In other words, you need to remove all non-numeric characters from the phone numbers. You can do this using Find and Replace to repeatedly remove each non-numeric character, such as dashes, periods, parentheses, etc. Once the phone numbers are clean, you can format them as phone numbers (using the Format Cells sequence mentioned earlier in this tip) and use the conditional formatting just described.

Conditionally Formatting Non-Integers

Makik has a list of numeric values. Some are integers; some have digits to the right of the decimal. He would like to use conditional formatting to highlight those values that have digits to the right of the decimal point.

There are a large number of ways that this can be done, and a number of different approaches. I won't go into how to define a conditional format here; such information has already been covered in other issues of ***ExcelTips***. Instead I'll focus on the condition itself and how you should select the condition to test.

If you know that the list will only contain numeric values, then you could use any number of formulas to determine whether the value is a non-integer. These are just a few that can be used if you specify that the condition contains a formula:

- =MOD(A1,1)>0
- =A1<>INT(A1)
- =A1-INT(A1)>0
- =NOT(A1=INT(A1))

- =(A1-TRUNC(A1))>0
- =ABS(A1)-INT(ABS(A1))>0
- =IF(FIND(".",A1),1,0)
- =(A1-(ROUNDDOWN(A1,0))>0)

The various formulas (and there could be many more listed) basically check to see if the unaltered value in the cell is equal to a version that makes sure there is nothing to the right of the decimal.

If you prefer (for some reason) to not rely upon a formula to define your condition, then you can choose "cell value is greater than" and set the condition as ROUNDDOWN(A1,0). You could also use "not equal to" in the condition and you could change ROUNDDOWN to ROUNDUP. Either way, you are testing to determine whether a rounded version of the number (rounded to the nearest integer) is equal to the original value or not.

You should note that any integer value in your list is formatted with decimal places, then such a value won't be "caught" by these conditional formats. For instance, if a cell contains the value 41 but the cell is formatted to display the value as 41.00, that value won't be "marked" by the conditional format as having something to the right of the decimal point. The reason is that the value really is an integer; it is just the display that adds the decimal point and two zeros.

Changing Excel's Background Color

The standard background color in Excel is white. You may, at some time, want to change the background color to something else, such as a light grey. Unfortunately, there is no way to change the background color; it is not a configurable option in Excel. There are a few things you can try as workarounds, however.

One approach involves selecting all the cells in the worksheet and applying a fill color to the cells. If you don't want the color to print, then you simply need to select all the cells and remove the fill color. This could be automated by using a macro to do the color removal, printing, and re-application.

There are drawbacks to such an approach, however. First, the colors used to fill the cells could interfere with the successful application of conditional formatting, if the conditional formatting involves the use of fill colors. (Conditional formatting applied to font specifications shouldn't be a problem.)

Another option is to create, in your favorite graphics program, a small rectangle that matches the color you want used for your background. Save the small rectangle as a graphics file, using the JPG file format. Then, within Excel, follow these steps:

1. Display the Page Layout tab of the ribbon.
2. In the Page Setup group, click the Background tool. Excel displays the Sheet Background dialog box.

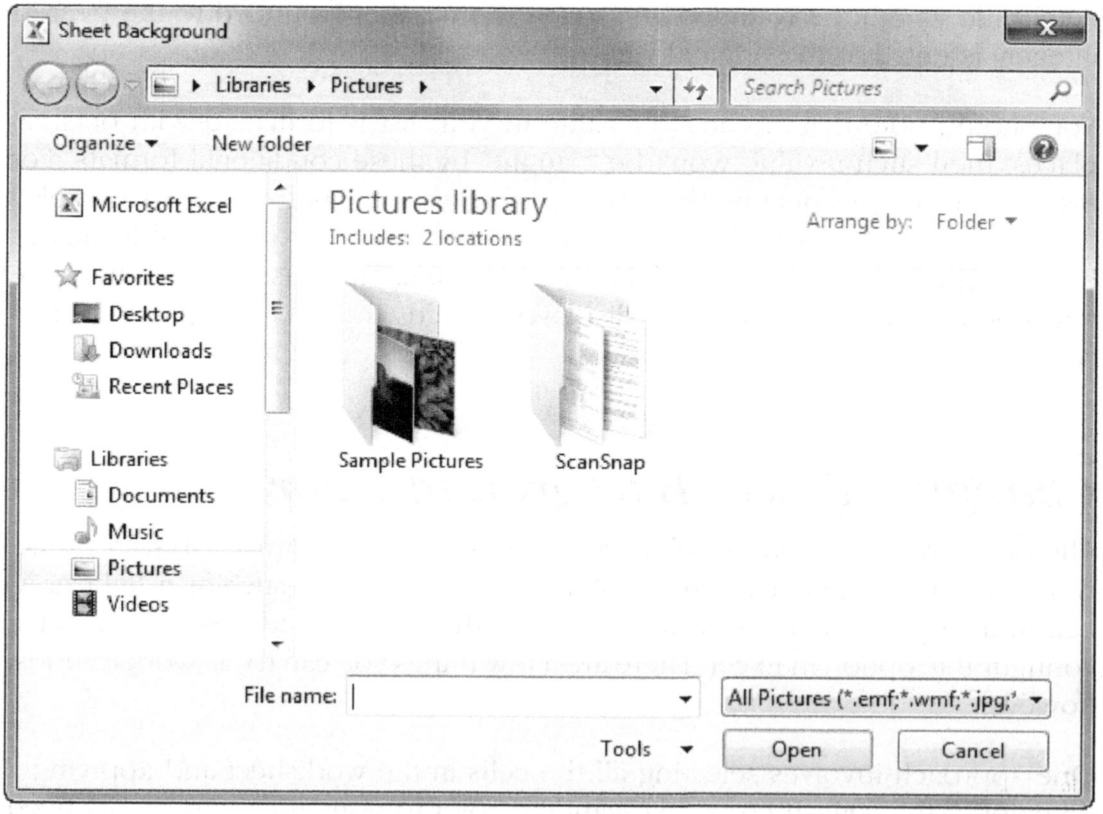

The Sheet Background dialog box.

2. Use the controls in the dialog box to locate and select the graphic image you created.
3. Click on OK.

The graphic image is placed in the background and repeated over and over again so that it fills the entire background. The benefit to this approach is that it doesn't affect any conditional formatting, and the background image won't print.

Speaking of conditional formatting, if you aren't using conditional formatting for any purpose in a worksheet, you could use it to create your background. In a blank area of your workbook, define a cell that contains the value True. Then select your worksheet that you want to have the background color, and use a conditional format to define that color. The format can look at the cell you defined, and if it is True then the color is applied. If the cell is not True then the color is not applied. This allows you to turn the background color on or off (for printing) by changing the value of a single cell.

You could also define styles for use in your worksheet. Define a style that has the desired background color, and another that does not. You can then apply the colored style when editing and the non-colored style when preparing to print.

5

Advanced Considerations

Conditional Format that Checks for Data Type

Joshua is trying to establish a conditional format that will alert a user that text data has been entered into a cell intended for numerical data or when numerical data has been input into a cell intended for text data.

A conditional format can be used to draw attention to when an improper value (text or numeric) has been entered in a cell, but a more robust approach might be to prohibit the improper value from being entered in the first place. This can be done with the data validation capabilities of Excel. These capabilities have been discussed, in detail, in other ***ExcelTips;*** more information can be found here:

`http://excel.tips.net/E165_Data_Validation.html`

Using data validation you can specify the type and range of data permitted in a cell, along with how stringently you want that specification followed. If you prefer to not use data validation for some reason, you can set up a conditional format that will verify if the information placed in a cell is of the data type you want. Follow these steps:

1. Select the cells that you want conditionally formatted.
2. With the Home tab of the ribbon displayed, click the Conditional Formatting option in the Styles group. Excel displays a palette of options related to conditional formatting.

3. Choose Highlight Cells Rules and then choose More Rules from the resulting submenu. Excel displays the New Formatting Rule dialog box.

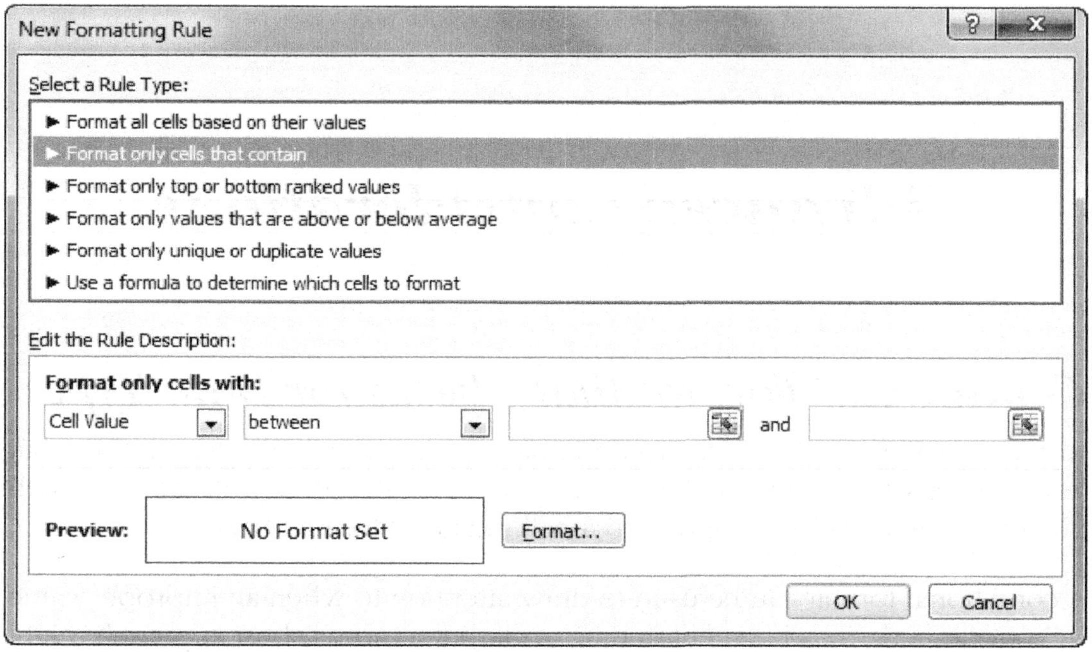

The New Formatting Rule dialog box.

4. In the Select a Rule Type area at the top of the dialog box, choose Use a Formula to Determine Which Cells to Format.
5. In the Format Values Where This Formula Is True box, enter one of the following formulas. (The first is if you want to highlight the cell if it contains text; the second if it contains a number. Make sure you replace A1 with the cell address of the cell in the upper-left corner of the range selected in step 1.)

```
=ISTEXT(A1)
=ISNUMBER(A1)
```

6. Click Format to display the Format Cells dialog box.
7. Using the controls in the dialog box, specify a format that you want used for those cells selected in step 1. For instance, you may want bold text in a red typeface.

8. Click OK to dismiss the Format Cells dialog box. The formatting you specified in step 7 should now appear in the preview area for the rule.
9. Click OK.

Conditional Formats that Distinguish Blanks and Zeroes

Let's say that you routinely import information from another program into Excel. The information contains numeric values, but it can also contain blanks. You might want to use a conditional format on the imported information to highlight any zero values. The problem is, if you just add a conditional format that highlights the cells to see if they are zero, then the condition will also highlight any cells that are blank, since they contain a "zero" value, as well.

There are several different solutions to this predicament. One solution is to apply a conditional format that uses two conditions. The first condition checks for the blanks, and the second checks for zero values. The condition that checks for blanks doesn't need to adjust any formatting, but the one that checks for zero values can. This works because if the first condition is satisfied (the cell is blank), the second condition is never tested. The following steps can implement the two-condition approach:

1. Select the range you want conditionally formatted. (For this example, I'll assume that you've selected the range A2:A99.)
2. With the Home tab of the ribbon displayed, click the Conditional Formatting option in the Styles group. Excel displays a palette of options related to conditional formatting.
3. Click Manage Rules. Excel displays the Conditional Formatting Rules Manager dialog box.
4. Click New Rule. Excel displays the New Formatting Rule dialog box.
5. In the Select a Rule Type area at the top of the dialog box, choose Format Only Cells That Contain.

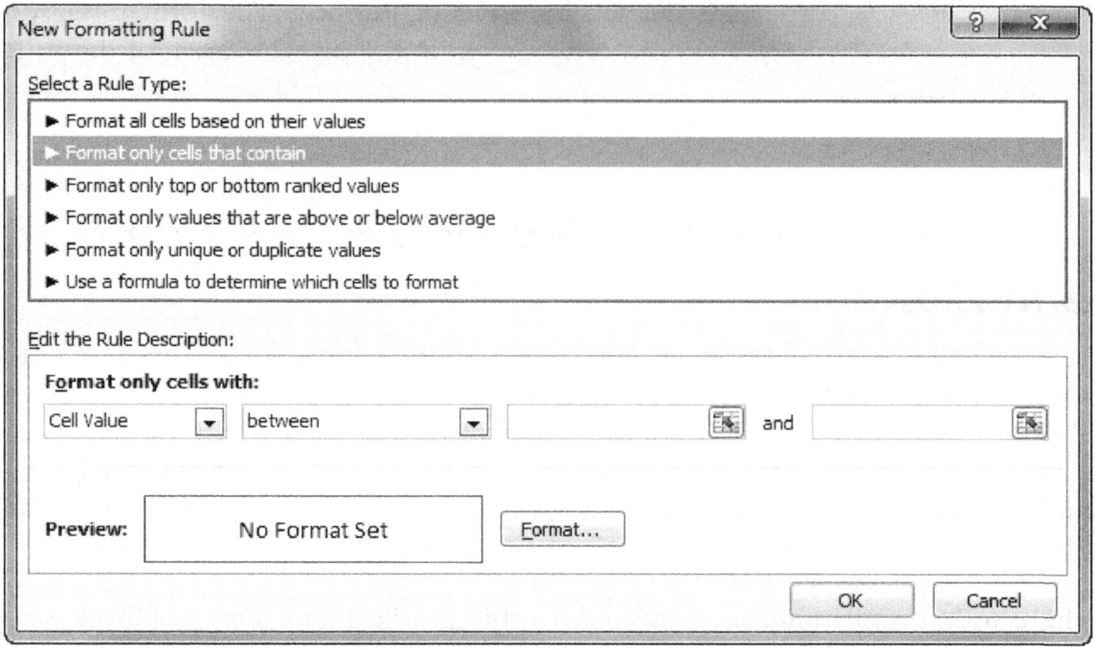

The New Formatting Rule dialog box.

6. Using the first drop-down list for the rule, choose Blanks.
7. Click OK. Excel closes the New Formatting Rule dialog box and again displays the Conditional Formatting Rules Manager dialog box, this time with your new rule visible. (Note that you didn't specify any formatting for this rule; that's fine.)
8. Make sure the Stop If True check box is selected for the rule.
9. Click New Rule. Excel again displays the New Formatting Rule dialog box.
10. In the Select a Rule Type area at the top of the dialog box, choose Format Only Cells That Contain.
11. Using the first drop-down list for the rule, choose Cell Value.
12. Using the second drop-down list for the rule, choose Equal To.
13. In the value box for Condition 2, enter **0**.

14. Click the Format button. Excel displays the Format Cells dialog box.
15. Use the controls in the dialog box to modify the formatting, as desired.
16. Click OK to close the Format Cells dialog box.
17. Click OK to close the New Formatting Rule dialog box. Excel again displays the Conditional Formatting Rules Manager, and the rule you just defined is the first one in the list. (It should also be selected.)
18. Click the down arrow to move the rule you just created to the second position in the list of rules.
19. Click OK to close the Conditional Formatting Rules Manager dialog box. The formatting is applied to the range of cells you selected in step 1.

Another solution is to combine your two conditions into a single condition. Follow these steps:

1. Select the range you want conditionally formatted. (For this example, I'll assume that you've selected the range A2:A99.)
2. With the Home tab of the ribbon displayed, click the Conditional Formatting option in the Styles group. Excel displays a palette of options related to conditional formatting.
3. Click New Rule. Excel displays the New Formatting Rule dialog box.
4. In the Select a Rule Type area at the top of the dialog box, choose Use a Formula To Determine Which Cells to Format.
5. In the formula box for Condition 1, enter this formula:

   ```
   =AND(A2=0,A2<>"").
   ```

6. Click the Format button. Excel displays the Format Cells dialog box.

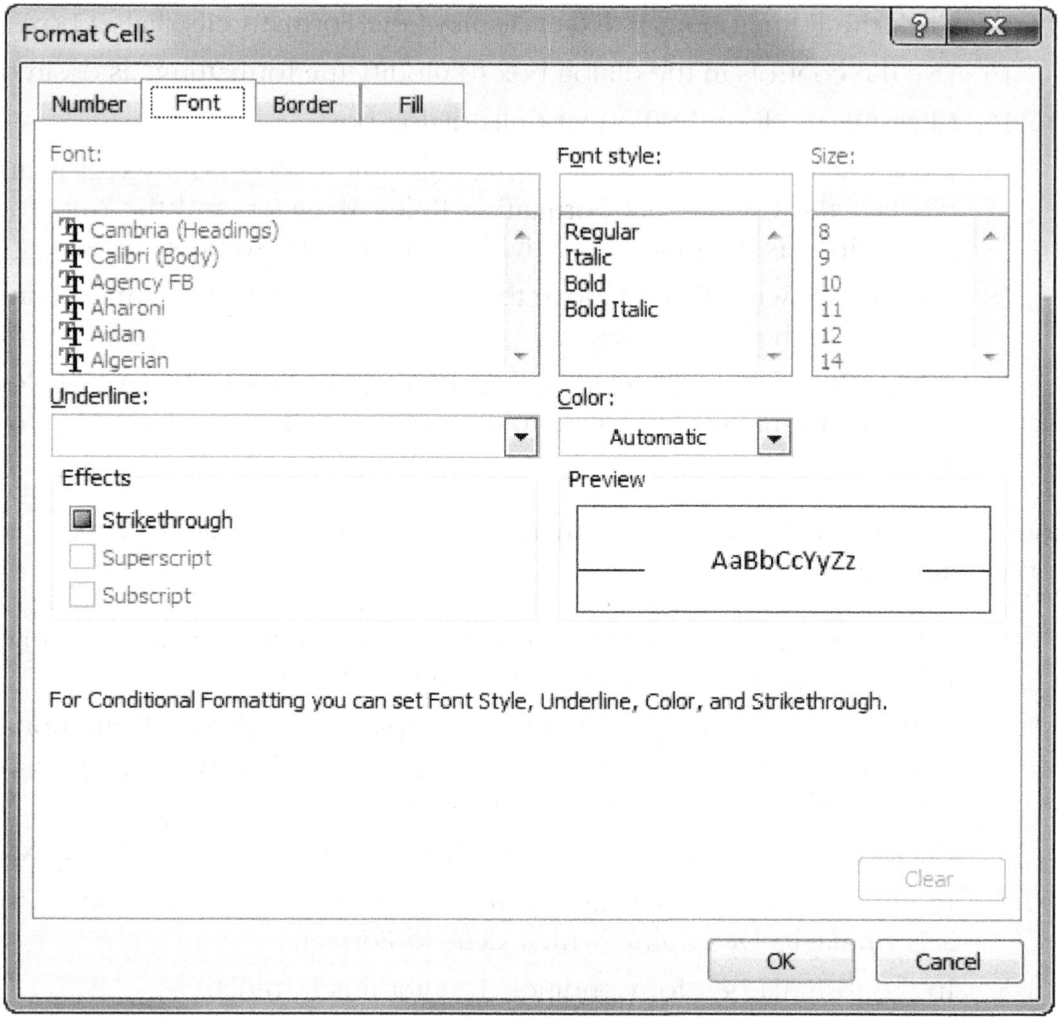

The Format Cells dialog box.

7. Use the controls in the dialog box to modify the formatting, as desired.
8. Click OK to close the Format Cells dialog box.
9. Click OK to close the New Formatting Rule dialog box. The formatting is applied to the range of cells you selected in step 1.

The formula used in step 5 checks to make sure that the value is 0 and that the cell is not blank. The AND function makes sure that only when both criteria are satisfied will the formula return True and the format be applied.

There are any number of other formulas that could also be used. For instance, each of the following formulas could be substituted in step 5:

- =AND(COUNT(A2)=1,A2=0)
- =AND(A2=0,NOT(ISBLANK(A2)))
- =AND(A2=0,LEN(A2)>0)
- =NOT(ISBLANK(A2))*(A2=0)

If you wanted an even faster way to highlight zero values while ignoring blanks, you might consider using a macro. The macro would be faster because you could just import and run it; you don't have to select a range of cells and enter the formula (or formulas) for the conditional formatting. The following macro is an example of one you could use:

```
Sub FormatRed()
    TotalRows = 65000
    ColNum = 1

    For i = 1 To Cells(TotalRows, ColNum).End(xlUp).Row
        Cells(i, ColNum).Interior.ColorIndex = xlAutomatic
        If IsNumeric(Cells(i, ColNum).Value) Then
            If Cells(i, ColNum).Value = 0 Then
                Cells(i, ColNum).Interior.ColorIndex = 3
            End If
        End If
    Next
End Sub
```

The macro checks the cells in column A. (It checks the cells in rows 1 through 65,000; you can modify this, if desired, to a larger number of rows.) If the cell contains a numeric value and that value is zero, then the cell is filled with red. If the cell contains something else, then the cell is set back to its normal color.

Counting Colors from Conditional Formats

Ronald has a worksheet that utilizes conditional formatting. The conditions result in the cells being different colors. He wants to count the number of cells that are red in the worksheet. He knows how to create a macro that will examine the cell color and do a count if a cell is formatted directly as red, but the macro won't work with cells that are conditionally formatted. Ronald wants to know if there is a way to count these conditionally red cells, as well.

You cannot directly check in a macro what the color of a cell is based on a conditional format. There are ways you can work around this with a macro, but it is not for the faint-of-heart. The following page on Chip Pearson's site demonstrates the difficulty in determining conditional colors:

```
http://www.cpearson.com/excel/CFColors.htm
```

Given the difficulty of the task, it may just be easier to recreate the conditions within the macro, and then see which cells meet these conditions. The result is that you count cells matching conditions rather than count cells that are colored red as a result of those conditions. This should yield the same count of cells, but is much easier to handle programmatically.

Of course, the only caveat to this solution is that you will need to keep the conditions in the macro and the conditions in the conditional formats in sync with each other. If you change one and fail to change the other, then you won't get the desired results.

Changing Font Face and Size Conditionally

Robin asks if there is a way to use Excel's conditional formatting capabilities to change the font used in a cell or to change the font size in a cell. The short answer is no, that can't be done—at least not with conditional formatting. (The controls that allow you to specify font name and size are grayed-out in the formatting dialog box used with conditional formatting.)

You can, however, use a macro to examine cell contents and make changes in the appearance of a cell. Consider the following macro, which examines any cells you have selected when you run the macro. If any of the cells have a length of more than two characters or a value of more than 10, then the cell's font is changed.

```
Sub DoReformat()
    Dim rCell As Range

    For Each rCell In Selection.Cells
        If Len(rCell.Text) > 2 Or _
          Val(rCell.Value) > 10 Then
            rCell.Font.Name = "Arial"
            rCell.Font.Size = 16
        Else
            rCell.Font.Name = "Times New Roman"
            rCell.Font.Size = 12
        End If
    Next
End Sub
```

To use the macro, just select the cells you want changed and then run the macro. If you want the formatting to change more automatically, then you can have the macro check to see if a change was made within a certain range of cells:

```
Private Sub Worksheet_Calculate()
    Dim rng As Range
    Dim rCell As Range

    Set rng = Range("A1:A10")

    For Each rCell In rng
        If Len(rCell.Text) > 2 Or _
          Val(rCell.Value) > 10 Then
            rCell.Font.Name = "Arial"
            rCell.Font.Size = 16
        Else
            rCell.Font.Name = "Times New Roman"
            rCell.Font.Size = 12
        End If
    Next
End Sub
```

This macro, when added to the worksheet object, will run every time the worksheet is recalculated. It checks the range A1:A10, applying the same tests as in the previous macro. The result is that the formatting of the cells is checked and changed continuously. To have the macro check a different range, just change the addresses assigned to the rng variable near the beginning of the macro.

One drawback of this macro is that it can get sluggish if you have a very large range for it to check. It will go very quickly if you are checking A1:A10 (ten cells), but may go much slower if you are continually checking B2:N465 (over 6,000 cells). In that case, you may want to design the macro so it runs whenever the worksheet is changed, but only takes action if the change was done to a cell in your target range. The following version is also added to the worksheet object:

```
Private Sub Worksheet_Change(ByVal Target As Range)
    Dim rCell As Range

    If Union(Target, Range("A1:A10")).Address = _
      Range("A1:A10").Address Then
        Application.EnableEvents = False
        For Each rCell In Target
            If Len(rCell.Text) > 2 Or _
              Val(rCell.Value) > 10 Then
                rCell.Font.Name = "Arial"
                rCell.Font.Size = 16
            Else
                rCell.Font.Name = "Times New Roman"
                rCell.Font.Size = 12
            End If
        Next
        Application.EnableEvents = True
    End If
End Sub
```

The macro uses the Union function to check whether the cells changed (passed to the event handler in the Target variable) have any overlap with the range you want checked. If they do, then the checking is done on the cells in the Target range.

One thing to keep in mind with macros that affect formatting is that if you have conditional formatting applied to a cell that is also checked by a macro, the formatting in the conditional formatting takes precedence over the formatting in the macro. If your macro is changing font name and font size, this isn't a big concern because conditional formatting won't affect these attributes. However, if you change your macro to also change a different format attribute—such as cell color—and that attribute is also changed by the conditional format, then it won't look like the macro did anything because Excel uses the conditional formatting in preference to what the macro does.

Sorting or Filtering by Conditional Format Results

John asked if it is possible to sort or filter based on the conditional formatting in a range of cells. He has a list of values in column A and a list in column B. He created a conditional format that makes any values in column A that are also in column B appear as bold red, and he wanted to sort or filter by that result.

The short answer is that no, you cannot sort by conditional formatting results. Doing so is much more complex than one might think, as shown at this page on Chip Pearson's Web site:

```
http://www.cpearson.com/excel/CFColors.htm
```

The easiest answer is to simply recreate your conditional formula in column C, to the right of your two columns of data. The formula should return True or False, depending on whether the value in column A is found somewhere in column B. With the True/False value in column C, you can filter or sort based on what is there.

Moving Cell Borders when Sorting

Frank has a simple two-column table that contains random dates in the first column and the letters A through E in the second column. He formats the cell containing the letter C so it has a background color and a border around the cell. When Frank sorts the table according to what is in the first column, Excel moves the background color with the C cell, but it doesn't move the border. Frank wonders if there is a way to move both the color and border of a cell when sorting.

The solution is to change how you are doing your formatting. Excel provides two types of formatting that can be applied to cells—regular formatting and conditional formatting. If you apply regular formatting, then what moves when you sort can seem rather arbitrary. If you apply conditional formatting, then all the formatting applied by the condition (or conditions) will move with the cell when you sort.

So the answer to the question is to change how you do your formatting in this instance. Just apply a conditional format that modifies the border of the cell, and then you can sort in peace. (The condition you set could easily be one that is always True, and thus the formatting always applied.)

Leaving a Cell Value Unchanged If a Condition Is False

While using the IF function, Vineet wants to retain the old value in the cell if the condition is false. In other words, the value in a cell where the IF function is used should change only if the condition being tested by the IF function is true. By default, however, the IF function makes the value 0 if the condition is False.

The IF function can take up to three parameters. The first parameter is the comparison that is to be made, the second parameter is what should be returned if the comparison is true, and the third is what should be returned if the comparison is false. It is possible to leave off the last parameter, but if you do then Excel will return the value 0 if the comparison is false. (This is what Vineet is seeing returned by his IF function usage.)

The obvious solution, then, is to make sure that you provide the IF function with something that should be returned when the comparison is false. For instance, let's say that your formula is in cell B1 and you are comparing something in cell A1. The formula you use may look like this:

```
=IF(A1<10,"under ten",B1)
```

Note that the words "under ten" are returned if the value in A1 is less than 10. If this condition is not met, then the value in B1 is returned. Since this formula is in cell B1, this means that the previous value in the cell is returned if the condition is false.

It also means that the formula contains a circular reference. For circular references to work OK you need to let Excel know that it is OK for them to occur in your worksheet. Choose Tools | Options | Calculation tab and make sure the Iteration check box is selected. Excel will now allow the circular reference without complaint.

If you don't want to allow a circular reference in your worksheet, then the only recourse is to create a macro that updates the value in cell B1 based upon any changes to cell A1:

```
Private Sub Workbook_SheetChange(ByVal Sh As Object, _
  ByVal Target As Range)

    ' See if the change is related to our cell
    If Not (Application.Intersect(Target, Range("A1")) _
      Is Nothing) Then
        If Range("A1") < 10 Then
            Range("B1") = "under ten"
        End If
    End If
End Sub
```

This simple macro, when added to the ThisWorkbook module, is executed every time there is a change in the workbook. If the value is cell A1 is changed (and only that cell), then the value is checked to see if it is less than 10. If it is, then the value in cell B1 is changed. If it isn't, then the value in cell B1 is left alone.

There is one "gottcha" that you need to keep in mind with any of the approaches discussed thus far, formula or macro. If the value in cell A1 is (let's say) 15, then cell B1 will contain what was there before, whatever it was. If you change the value in cell A1 to (let's say) 7, then B1 will change to "under ten." That's fine, but from that point on cell B1 will never appear to change. Why? Because if you then change cell A1 to a value greater than 10, cell B1 will contain (as just explained) what was there before. And, as you now understand, the value that was there before is the result of the previous true result, which was "under ten." Thus, true or false, the formula or macro from this point on displays the text "under ten."

Removing Conditional Formats, but Not the Effects

Charlie wondered if there is a way to "make permanent" the effects of conditional formatting at any given time. For instance, if a conditional format specifies that a particular cell be bold red type, then Charlie wanted a way to remove the conditional format and make the cell bold and red.

There is no intrinsic way to do this in Excel; none of the Paste Special options will do the task, as desired. You can, however, use a macro to accomplish the task:

```
Option Explicit
Sub PasteFC()
    Application.ScreenUpdating = False
    Dim rWhole As Range
    Dim rCell As Range
    Dim ndx As Integer
    Dim FCFont As Font
    Dim FCBorder As Border
    Dim FCInt As Interior
    Dim x As Integer
    Dim iBorders(3) As Integer

    iBorders(0) = xlLeft
    iBorders(1) = xlRight
    iBorders(2) = xlTop
    iBorders(3) = xlBottom

    Set rWhole = Selection

    For Each rCell In rWhole
        rCell.Select
        ndx = ActiveCondition(rCell)
        If ndx <> 0 Then
            'Change the Font info
            Set FCFont = rCell.FormatConditions(ndx).Font
            With rCell.Font
                .Bold = NewFC(.Bold, FCFont.Bold)
                .Italic = NewFC(.Italic, FCFont.Italic)
                .Underline = NewFC(.Underline, FCFont.Underline)
                .Strikethrough = NewFC(.Strikethrough, _
                  FCFont.Strikethrough)
                .ColorIndex = NewFC(.ColorIndex, FCFont.ColorIndex)
            End With
            'Change the Border Info for each of the 4 types
            For x = 0 To 3
```

```
                Set FCBorder = rCell.FormatConditions(ndx).
Borders(iBorders(x))
                With rCell.Borders(iBorders(x))
                    .LineStyle = NewFC(.LineStyle, FCBorder.LineStyle)
                    .Weight = NewFC(.Weight, FCBorder.Weight)
                    .ColorIndex = NewFC(.ColorIndex, FCBorder.ColorIndex)
                End With
            Next x
            'Change the interior info
            Set FCInt = rCell.FormatConditions(ndx).Interior
            With rCell.Interior
                .ColorIndex = NewFC(.ColorIndex, FCInt.ColorIndex)
                .Pattern = NewFC(.Pattern, FCInt.Pattern)
            End With
            'Delete FC
            rCell.FormatConditions.Delete
        End If
    Next
    rWhole.Select
    Application.ScreenUpdating = True
    MsgBox ("The Formatting based on the Conditions" & vbCrLf & _
      "in the range " & rWhole.Address & vbCrLf & _
      "has been made standard for those cells" & vbCrLf & _
      "and the Conditional Formatting has been removed")
End Sub

Function NewFC(vCurrent As Variant, vNew As Variant)
    If IsNull(vNew) Then
        NewFC = vCurrent
    Else
        NewFC = vNew
    End If
End Function

Function ActiveCondition(rng As Range) As Integer
    'Chip Pearson http://www.cpearson.com/excel/CFColors.htm
    Dim ndx As Long
    Dim FC As FormatCondition

    If rng.FormatConditions.Count = 0 Then
        ActiveCondition = 0
    Else
    For ndx = 1 To rng.FormatConditions.Count
        Set FC = rng.FormatConditions(ndx)
        Select Case FC.Type
            Case xlCellValue
                Select Case FC.Operator
                    Case xlBetween
                        If CDbl(rng.Value) >= CDbl(FC.Formula1) And _
                          CDbl(rng.Value) <= CDbl(FC.Formula2) Then
                            ActiveCondition = ndx
                            Exit Function
                        End If
```

```
                    Case xlGreater
                        If CDbl(rng.Value) > CDbl(FC.Formula1) Then
                            ActiveCondition = ndx
                            Exit Function
                        End If
                    Case xlEqual
                        If CDbl(rng.Value) = CDbl(FC.Formula1) Then
                            ActiveCondition = ndx
                            Exit Function
                        End If
                    Case xlGreaterEqual
                        If CDbl(rng.Value) >= CDbl(FC.Formula1) Then
                            ActiveCondition = ndx
                            Exit Function
                        End If
                    Case xlLess
                        If CDbl(rng.Value) < CDbl(FC.Formula1) Then
                            ActiveCondition = ndx
                            Exit Function
                        End If
                    Case xlLessEqual
                        If CDbl(rng.Value) <= CDbl(FC.Formula1) Then
                            ActiveCondition = ndx
                            Exit Function
                        End If
                    Case xlNotEqual
                        If CDbl(rng.Value) <> CDbl(FC.Formula1) Then
                            ActiveCondition = ndx
                            Exit Function
                        End If
                    Case xlNotBetween
                        If CDbl(rng.Value) <= CDbl(FC.Formula1) Or _
                            CDbl(rng.Value) >= CDbl(FC.Formula2) Then
                            ActiveCondition = ndx
                            Exit Function
                        End If
                    Case Else
                        Debug.Print "UNKNOWN OPERATOR"
                End Select
            Case xlExpression
                If Application.Evaluate(FC.Formula1) Then
                    ActiveCondition = ndx
                    Exit Function
                End If
            Case Else
                Debug.Print "UNKNOWN TYPE"
        End Select
    Next ndx
    End If
    ActiveCondition = 0
End Function
```

There are three procedures in this solution. The last procedure, ActiveCondition, is designed to return a number indicating which of the conditions in a conditional format is currently in effect. This routine was found at Chip Pearson's site, as indicated in the first comment of the function. (No sense in re-inventing the wheel. <g>)

The center function, NewFC, is simply used to determine which of two values is valid. The procedure you actually run, however, is PasteFC. Simply select the cells you want to convert to explicit formatting, then run the procedure. It checks each cell you selected for which formatting condition is active, determines the formatting of that condition, and then applies it to the cell. Finally, the conditional formatting for the cell is removed.

Conditional Formatting with Data Imported from Access

Cory is having a problem getting his conditional formatting to work as desired with information imported into Excel from Access. The data being imported in a particular column can either be text (such as "17 U") or numeric (such as 32). The conditional format checks to see if the value in the cell is greater than zero, in which case the value is underlined. This won't work properly with the imported data because not only does Excel treat the text (17 U) as text, but it also treats the numeric (32) as text. This makes sense, since Excel treats the entire column as text rather than changing data format for each cell in the column.

There are a couple of ways you can fix this problem. One is to change the formula you are using in your conditional format. Instead of checking to see if the value is greater than zero, use the following formula (set the conditional check to "Format Is"):

```
=VALUE(E3) > 0
```

This formula uses the VALUE function to check what is in cell E3. If the contents are a number—even if it is formatted as text by Excel—then the formula returns True and the condition is met for the formatting. If the contents of E3 really are text (as in "17 U"), then the formula returns a #VALUE error, which does not satisfy the condition and the formatting is not applied.

Another approach is to force Excel to evaluate the imported cells and convert them to numeric values, if appropriate. An easy way to do this is as follows:

1. After importing the data, select a blank cell from a column outside the range of those you just imported.
2. Press **Ctrl+C**. This copies the contents of the cell (nothing) to the Clipboard.
3. Select the cells that you want evaluated by Excel. For instance, select the column that contains the text values and the numeric values formatted as text.
4. Display the Home tab of the ribbon.
5. Click the down-arrow under the Paste tool, and then choose Paste Special. Excel displays the Paste Special dialog box.

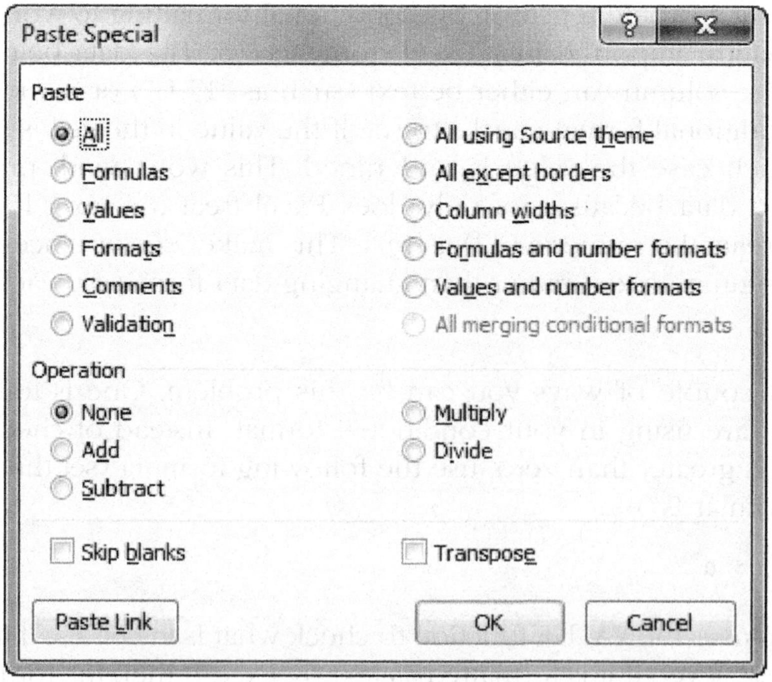

The Paste Special dialog box.

6. Click the Add radio button.
7. Click OK.

What you just did was to "add" the contents of the Clipboard to all the cells you selected in step 3. If the cells contained real text, then nothing happened to those cells; they remain the same and are still treated as text. If the cells contained a numeric value, then Excel treats it as a number and adds zero to it. This value, as a numeric, is deposited back in the cell, and treated as a real number. This means that the conditional formatting test that you previously set up should work just fine on those cells since they are no longer treated as text.

Checking All Cell Formatting in VBA

Excel has two different types of formatting that can be applied to cell. The first is explicit formatting. This type of formatting is applied by using the tools on the various ribbons for by using the Format Cells dialog box. The second type of formatting is conditional formatting. This type of formatting is applied based on a set of rules that you define.

It is important to understand that these two types of formatting are separate and distinct from each other. For instance, if you explicitly format a cell as bold red, that is the way it appears. If you later apply a conditional format to it, and that format causes the cell to appear in green, that is exactly what is happening—the cell is ***appearing*** in green, but it is still formatted as red.

What does this have to do with VBA? If you test the formatting of a cell in VBA, then the formatting you are testing is the explicit formatting. In the above scenario, this means that the test will always indicate that the cell is bold red, and never report that it is green, regardless of what the conditional formatting is doing to the cell. This is because conditional formatting affects the cell's display, not its underlying (explicit) formatting.

The other upshot of all this is that if you want to find out what conditional formatting is being displayed, you may need to recreate all your conditional tests within VBA. This can get rather complex rather quickly. For more information on this topic, there is a great page you can refer to. Check out one of Chip Pearson's pages, here:

```
http://www.cpearson.com/excel/CFColors.htm
```

Conditionally Playing an Audio File

Tassos would like to have Excel play an audio file when the value in a certain cell exceeds a threshold. For instance, when the value in a cell exceeds 999 he would like a particular sound file to be played.

There is no built-in way to do this in Excel (although it would be an interesting addition to Excel's conditional formatting features). You can, however, play a sound file by using a macro to do a call to the Windows API.

You need to start by placing some code in the Sheet object for the workbook. (Right-click the tab for the worksheet and choose View Code from the Context menu.) Declare the function "playsound" using the following code:

```
Private Declare Function PlaySound Lib "winmm.dll" _
  Alias "PlaySoundA" (ByVal lpszName As String, _
  ByVal hModule As Long, ByVal dwFlags As Long) As Long

    Const SND_SYNC = &H0
    Const SND_ASYNC = &H1
    Const SND_FILENAME = &H20000
```

Next you can create a short little macro that will actually play the sound file. Assuming that the sound file is in the same directory as the workbook, the following code will work. (You should modify the code so that it contains the proper filename and location.)

```
Sub PlayWAV()
    WAVFile = ThisWorkbook.Path & "\MyAudioFile.wav"
    Call PlaySound(WAVFile, 0&, SND_ASYNC Or SND_FILENAME)
End Sub
```

Finally, establish the criteria when the file is to be played. In this case you want the sound file to play whenever the value in the target cell exceeds the threshold value of 999. The following will check for that condition in cell C5 and, if warranted, play the sound file:

```
Private Sub Worksheet_Change(ByVal Target As Range)
    Threshold = 999
    If Range("C5").Value > Threshold Then PlayWAV
End Sub
```

Now, whenever the value in Cell C5 changes and exceeds 999, the audio file will play one time. If the value is changed to less than 999, nothing plays. If the value changes to another value that exceeds 999, the sound file will play again.

For additional ideas on playing audio files, check out these sites:

```
http://www.j-walk.com/ss/excel/tips/tip87.htm
http://www.cpearson.com/excel/PlaySound.aspx
```

You should note, as well, that you can get Excel to play a system sound by using data validation. Simply set up the validation criteria (described in other issues of ***ExcelTips***) and then, on the Error tab, specify whether you want Excel to stop, warn, or inform the user. When a value is entered in the cell that does not fit the criteria, a dialog box is displayed and the system sound is heard.

Discover the Power in Excel!

Books, e-books, and CDs from Tips.Net

Amazing Array Formulas

An array is a group of items that can, in some fashion, be treated as a whole. In Excel, an array formula is a special type of formula that allows you to perform calculations on huge amounts of data, in a single operation. Array formulas, once properly understood, provide new and exciting ways that you can perform calculations with your data—some that would otherwise be impossible with regular Excel formulas.

In the pages of *ExcelTips: Amazing Array Formulas* you'll discover not only what array functions are and how to create them, but also dozens of different ways you can use them right away.

Excel 2007 Conditional Formatting

The conditional formatting capabilities of Excel are impressive and can be very powerful. All you need to do is picture how you want your data to appear, and then figure out the criteria that should be met in order for the formatting to be applied. Whenever the values change on which your conditional formatting is based, Excel changes the formatting to reflect those changed values.

Excel allows most of its formatting power to be applied based on the criteria you dream up. *Excel 2007 Conditional Formatting* presents everything you need to know to put conditional formatting to work with your data.

Excel 2010 Filters and Filtering

Filtering your data means displaying only a part of it. You provide the criteria that Excel should use to determine what gets displayed, and Excel helpfully displays just that data. Filtering is especially useful if you have a large data list and you want to work with only a subset of the records in that list.

Excel 2010 Filters and Filtering helps you manage your data effectively and efficiently. It provides the information you need to understand how both of Excel's filtering tools work and how you can use those tools with the real-world data you need to process. Get a grip on your data with *Excel 2010 Filters and Filtering!*

Excel 2007 Graphics and Charts

Many people, especially when they are new to Excel, create worksheets that contain only numbers, text, and formulas. Excel worksheets can contain much more than these elemental items. You can add all sorts of graphics to your worksheets or you can create amazing charts from your data. These items—graphics and charts—can liven up your data and provide some exciting ways to make your information mean even more.

Excel 2007 Graphics and Charts focuses on what you need to know to understand and put graphics and charts to work right away. You'll discover ways to stretch your knowledge and enhance how you can present the data in your worksheets.

Excel 2010 PivotTables for the Faint of Heart

For many people, the mere mention of "PivotTables" sends shivers up their spine. To some, the PivotTable is one of those tools in Excel that is best left some mythical (and mystical) expert, perhaps locked away in some ivory tower. For such folks, the PivotTable remains the most esoteric and exotic of Excel's analysis tools.

PivotTables don't need to be so scary, and they certainly don't need to be relegated to the realm of the esoteric or exotic. With *Excel 2010 PivotTables for the Faint of Heart* you can start using PivotTables right away to crunch the numbers you need to crunch and discover the answers hidden in your data.

Visit http://store.tips.net for more great Tips.Net titles!

Excel 2010 Serious Sorting

Using Excel you can manage data in a variety of ways with a number of tools. One commonly used Excel tool is embodied within its sorting capabilities. Excel allows you to easy and quickly sort data in just about any manner you can conceive.

Even though sorting data may be a routine task in Excel, many people still don't have a firm grasp on how to use the program's sorting capabilities fully. Even those who have been using the program for years and years often get into a rut and fail to recognize or take advantage of the full sorting power inherent in Excel.

Excel 2010 Serious Sorting discusses how you can use all the sorting capabilities provided in Excel, perhaps in ways you've never before considered.

ExcelTips: The Macros

Want to master Excel and make it adapt to what you want done? Then you need to discover the power of macros. Macros are a great way to expand the utility of Excel and the ways you can use the program.

ExcelTips: The Macros is designed for those wanting to learn how to create, use, and expand their understanding of Excel macros. In its pages you uncover how to make your use of Excel even more productive. It is the largest, most in-depth exploration of macros available anywhere!

Powerful Lookup Functions

Excel provides hundreds of worksheet functions you can use to build formulas, modify data, and get just the information you need in a cell. Of all the worksheet functions available, few are more powerful than Excel's lookup functions. They literally allow you to "look up" information based upon parameters you specify.

The pages of *ExcelTips: Powerful Lookup Functions* focus on dozens of tips that can help you better understand not only what lookup functions are, but how to use them in real-world scenarios to improve the calculations you must do in your own workbooks.

Times and Dates

Many people use Excel to enter, process, calculate, format, and display dates or times. *ExcelTips: Times and Dates* is designed to help you figure out just what to do with the times and dates stuck in your worksheets. No matter how you need to work with dates and times, *ExcelTips: Times and Dates* can help you out.

Stay in Top Form!

If you want to stay in top Excel form, consider subscribing to *ExcelTips*. Your subscription is free; all you need is an e-mail account and you can receive a weekly dose of tips related to Excel. To subscribe, just visit the *ExcelTips* Web site:

http://excelribbon.tips.net

If you need tips for older versions of Excel (Excel 97 through Excel 2003), then you'll want to visit our website that focuses on those versions:

http://excel.tips.net

ExcelTips is part of the Tips.Net network, a collection of websites designed to bring you helpful tips, tricks, and ideas that can save you time, effort, and money. You can see the full breadth of the Tips.Net network by visiting our website:

http://www.tips.net

Visit http://store.tips.net for more great Tips.Net titles!

Made in the USA
Monee, IL
08 November 2026

67858838R00070